Fishing with
My Father

Fishing with My Father

A Literary Companion

Edited by

Peter Kaminsky

CHAMBERLAIN BROS.

a member of Penguin Group (USA) Inc.

CHAMBERLAIN BROS.
Published by the Penguin Group
Penguin Group (USA) Inc., 375 Hudson Street, New York, New York 10014, USA
Penguin Group (Canada), 10 Alcorn Avenue, Toronto, Ontario M4V 3B2, Canada
(a division of Pearson Penguin Canada Inc.)
Penguin Books Ltd, 80 Strand, London WC2R 0RL, England
Penguin Ireland, 25 St Stephen's Green, Dublin 2, Ireland
(a division of Penguin Books Ltd)
Penguin Group (Australia), 250 Camberwell Road, Camberwell, Victoria 3124,
Australia (a division of Pearson Australia Group Pty Ltd)
Penguin Books India Pvt Ltd, 11 Community Centre, Panchsheel Park,
New Delhi–110 017, India
Penguin Group (NZ), Cnr Airborne and Rosedale Roads, Albany, Auckland 1310,
New Zealand (a division of Pearson New Zealand Ltd)
Penguin Books (South Africa) (Pty) Ltd, 24 Sturdee Avenue, Rosebank,
Johannesburg 2196, South Africa

Penguin Books Ltd, Registered Offices: 80 Strand, London WC2R 0RL, England

Contents

Fishing with
My Father

Introduction
In Praise of Small Moments

PETER KAMINSKY

I didn't fish with my dad when I was growing up for the simple reason that I didn't fish at all until my early twenties. Then fishing took over my life. Best thing I ever did, and just about all I ever wanted to do from then on. So between 1974 and the birth of my first child in 1985, had you asked me what my favorite pastime was, I would have answered in a nanosecond: "Fishing!"

I would now amend that to "Fishing with my daughter." I have two daughters and they are, of course, very different. The older one, Lucy, is the fisher. Her younger sister, Lily, has not taken to the sport with the same enthusiasm, although we have had some nice moments with rod and reel. Her fishing chapters may yet be written. Every kid is a whole new book, as the stories in this volume so richly show. It's a simple enough equation—fishing plus parent equals one fine memory—but for every child and every parent, the sum is always different.

Fishing with my daughter has made me a better man, and, I like to believe, it has made her a better fisher. Only with her will I sit in the back of a drift boat for hours as she tries to master the presentation of the dry fly. Then, when luck and art are with her, she will set the hook on some lovely trout or bass that foolishly ambushes it. With anybody else the sight of rising, catchable fish will motivate me to action, as strongly as the homing urge calls salmon upstream. But with my daughter, I gladly sit in the back, without a rod, watching her cast to gorgeous Montana trout until she gets the hang of it. Not fishing doesn't bother me a bit.

That doesn't make me a great dad but it does make me a different father than, say, Papa Hemingway. His son, Jack, was a friend of mine (as well as a contributor to this volume). Some years ago, he and I spent a fruitless week in Cuba chasing marlin, which neither of us very much cared about (but the filmmakers who had brought us there did). We passed the long, hot hours on ship drinking "red beer" (cold beer with equally cold tomato juice). We trolled flies for dolphin (dolphin fish, not Flipper) because we preferred fly-fishing. It certainly beat doing nothing, which is what the marlin-hunting amounted to.

I asked Jack why he wasn't turned on by marlin fishing. After all, they are huge creatures and they were the reason that his father had picked up the family and moved from Key

West to Havana (where it was a shorter boat ride to the marlin grounds) when he was young.

"You know what I don't like about it?" Jack said. "In all the years I went fishing with Papa, he offered me the rod exactly *once!*"

Had I spent my boyhood inhaling diesel fumes and trolling lures in ninety-degree heat in hopes that someone else would catch a fish . . . well, all I can say is, Papa Hemingway still had some learning to do in the fatherhood department. If my kid has a shot at a fish, I let her take it.

Having said that, I bet if you asked Lucy, she would be able to come up with two or three hundred instances when she was convinced that I nudged her out of the way for a cast. But I know in my heart that I truly have enjoyed being with her as she fished, even when I never lifted my rod.

Another thing I have learned to do—again probably less than I should have but more than I was inclined to—is to keep my mouth shut. Tell a kid—or anyone—what they are doing wrong every time they blow a cast (or anything else, from making a left-turn signal to over-salting a soup) and you will get tuned out, if not thoroughly resented. On the other hand, let a person make his or her own mistakes and you have a very good chance of speaking to an attentive listener when you do chime in.

Being a parent is a lot about *not* telling your kids what not to do. By the same measure, being a kid and maturing is a lot about learning that your parents occasionally can give good advice and that they have your best interests at heart.

In this regard, I often remind myself that fishing, in contrast to some other equally satisfying hobbies, is not merely *like* life; it is life. Whether or not you keep your catch or throw it back, fishing fulfills a basic drive: the search for food. When you fish, you are seeking to sustain life, yet at the same time you are seeking to deprive another creature of its own existence. This is a serious load of psychological freight—or at least heavy karma.

So although anything you do with your child purely for pleasure no doubt deepens the bonds of affection, I think fishing is special because it fulfills a primal urge. It is part of our Cro-Magnon DNA. I suppose golfers might attempt a similarly passionate brief for their sport. But golfing is, at best, a metaphor for life. Fishing is and always has been life itself. After all, have you ever seen a cave painting from 35,000 B.C. depicting someone teeing off on a par-five?

One of my favorite things about fishing with my children is that you can go a long time without talking but still feel that you are communicating. Drive somewhere with your child and you are liable to spend a good amount of time gabbing. Go with them to a restaurant and there's still more talk, much of it unmemorable. When you fish together, you are both on the same circuit, plugged into the world and feeling the juice.

Often, you are liable to be in a particularly beautiful spot. Such a place calms the soul, soothes the spirit. It quiets things down in the nicest way. You might very well be all alone, just the two of you, in your own wilderness. There is no practical reason to speak in hushed tones. There's no one within miles of earshot; but you speak softly anyway because the serenity of the scene works its way in your soul. The rhythm of the world slows and grows less insistent.

Somehow within the swath of grace in which fishing places its devotees, important questions that are only mentioned in rushed conversations in the everyday world, if at all, are easier to bring up: *What are you doing this summer? Did you have a problem getting that paper in on time? Any thoughts about grad school? A job?*

In our commonplace existence such questions often come across as parental nagging. On the water they are easier to bring up, probably because they are also easier to drop. I don't know why this is so, but it is. A passing loon, a vicious trout rise, a beaver paddling across the water, a pretty girl sunning herself on a rock (which I would notice) or a hunky guy diving into the water (that's more Lucy's department)—any of these things can move the conversation off of uncomfortable turf. While in the car or on the phone any answers to your queries would probably be met with the infuriating "I don't want to talk about it anymore," on the water you're more likely to be put off with "Ssh, Dad, there's a deer and two fawns over there!"

There's also a little parental image-burnishing that comes along with a father-daughter outing. Succeeding with a long cast and a skillful fight is wonderfully satisfying if your child is a witness. It makes up, just a little, for all the times that you fall short of setting an example as a competent adult. These angling triumphs offer the chance for a father to bask in the warmth of his child's admiration. Catching a fish means you have done something right. No matter how much the two of you might be prone to bickering, a caught fish is an indisputable fact of life, and it is one that we are hardwired to admire.

As time marches on and little boys and girls become men and women, fishing together becomes sharing the driving, having a beer together, eating a hamburger at 10:30 at night with one hand on the steering wheel, laughing at the big billboards in small towns that advertise themselves as "The Gooseberry Capital of the West," falling asleep in some so-so motel (not even changing out of your fishing clothes because you are dead tired), rolling out of bed when the alarm goes off for an early start on the water, sharing a breakfast of two Hershey bars and the semi-intact banana in your backpack . . . these simple pleasures are trivial when considered against the backdrop of war and peace, famine and earthquake. But somehow that one piece of chocolate, that fine stack of buckwheat cakes and chewy bacon, that ugly baseball hat that you bought at the Sunoco station after a malicious gust of wind absconded with your old favorite . . . somehow, all of these inconsequential events will be remembered much more clearly than politics and wars, or the comings and goings of the rich and powerful. People often say "the devil is in the details" and there is some truth to that. But as I have found in fishing with my child, it is equally true that there is divinity in all those details that make up the memories that the two of you—and only the two of you—can share about your times on the water.

But enough about me and my kids. The thing about fishing with fathers or sons or daughters is that I would bet every father's memories would be equally powerful and personally important in the way that mine are to me. In this book you will read about youngsters learning from fathers and about grown-ups learning to move on when fathers are no longer around. You will learn about taking advice and giving it. About the delicious days of summer when parents and their offspring all become kids for a few enchanted hours and the frosty days of winter when the company of kin provides all the warmth you need. And apart from all this moral uplift, I am reminded as I read these pieces of the best reason I know of to fish, or to do anything else . . . it's one of life's joys.

As Humphrey Bogart said to Ingrid Bergman, I would say to every child who goes fishing with Dad: "Here's looking at you, kid!"

Twiggling

*Landlocked salmon signify the start of spring
and the rituals that bind father and son.*

WILLIAM G. TAPPLY

In my family, the fishing season opened sometime in April with a phone call from Charley Watkins, who owned the housekeeping cabins on Sebago Lake in Maine. The old guy was quite deaf. He believed he had to yell in order to be heard, and if I was in the room when Dad answered his call, I had no trouble following Charley's end of the conversation.

"SHE'S CRACKED OPEN, MR. TAPPLY," he would scream as Dad held the phone away from his ear. "ICE WENT OUT THIS MORNIN'. YOU BOYS BETTER GIT YERSELVES ON UP HERE. I GOT A CABIN WAITIN' FOR YOU."

Dad would yell, "WE'LL BE THERE FRIDAY NIGHT," and Charley would scream, "WHAT'S THAT YOU SAY?" Dad would repeat himself, his face growing red, until Charley finally hollered, "WELL, SOMETHIN'S WRONG WITH OUR CONNECTION, BUT I'LL BE EXPECTIN' YOU AND THE BOYS ON FRIDAY NIGHT, OKAY?"

Dad was the landlocked-salmon Paul Revere, so after he hung up with Charley Watkins, he phoned the alert to Tom Craven and the Putnam brothers and Gorham Cross and his other old fishing partners, and to each of them he gave his own Charley Watkins imitation. "SEBAGO'S CRACKED OPEN. TIME TO GO FISHING AGAIN."

I sat patiently at the kitchen table, and when he'd finished his round of calls, Dad would look at me. "You can come if you want."

Of course I wanted to go.

landlocked salmon

Landlocked salmon were legendary gamefish to a young boy, and I knew all about them. Salmo salar sebago, they were called, after the lake where we fished for them and where the rod-and-reel record, a 22½-pounder, was taken in 1907. These salmon, biologically identical to their anadromous Atlantic brethren, spawned in rivers, but instead of migrating to the ocean, they spent their lives in the cold, clear lakes of Maine. Their main forage was smelt, which were abundant in these waters.

Landlocked-salmon fishing meant trolling smelt-imitation streamers and bucktails with evocative names for a young boy—Gray Ghost, Warden's Worry, Supervisor, Dark Edson Tiger, Black Nose Dace—over dropoffs along Sebago's rock-strewn shoreline, around the Dingley Islands, and back and forth across the mouth of the Songo River.

We rigged our heavy bamboo fly rods with a Dark Tiger—always a Dark Tiger—on the point of a long leader, with any of a dozen or more classic landlocked patterns for a dropper. Dad claimed that 90 percent of his salmon came to the Tiger, but landing a single salmon was always considered a triumph, so we never caught enough fish to constitute a valid sampling.

Wind, especially if accompanied by a cold rain, made for prime salmon trolling. Such days were, in fact, the norm for southern Maine in mid-April. We would drag short floating lines along the windward shoreline where, according to the theory, the baitfish got blown and churned around by the sloshing surf, making them disoriented and vulnerable to the predatory salmon.

When Sebago lay flat and glassy, we let out an entire sinking fly line, Dad would cut back the motor to its lowest speed, and I would lie back on my bow seat, tilt up my face, and close my eyes to the warmth of the sun. I don't recall ever getting a strike under such conditions. Those days we'd hope for a four o'clock blow. It was like duck hunting: The worst conditions made the best action. A salmon troller was supposed to welcome misery.

Wind was the key—but not just any wind. We believed utterly in the old New England folklore:

> When the wind is in the east,
> that's when salmon bite the least.
> When the wind is in the north,
> that's when fishermen set not forth.
> When the wind is in the west,
> that's when salmon bite the best.
> And when the wind is in the south,
> it blows the bait to the fish's mouth.

For the first few hours of the first morning of the new season, regardless of the conditions, I leaned tensely forward in my bow seat, facing back to where my fly line trailed out and disappeared behind the boat. I gripped my rod in both hands, expectant and alert, ready for whatever kind of salmon strike might come—a "tip-dipper" or "rod-bouncer" or "reel-screecher" or any of several subtle variations of each.

But actual strikes were rare, and when my high-strung boy's anticipation dulled, which it did rather quickly, I carved a trolling stick, wedged it in the gunnels, and rested my rod against it, on the well-documented theory that salmon were most likely to strike when you least expected it. Then I allowed my mind to wander on the hypnotic thrum of Dad's two-horse Evinrude, and I tried to recall those rare but magical times when my tip had dipped and my rod had bounced and my reel had screeched and behind us a silvery arc had exploded from the gray corrugated water that, only days earlier, had been ice.

When it actually happened, it was always a surprise. The rod bucked against the trolling stick, then bent acutely, and then the reel zizzed, and as I fumbled for it, a salmon leaped far out behind the boat.

Sometimes there was no leap. Then we had a delicious mystery on the end of the line—a "squaretail," maybe, a genuine native Maine brook trout, which often ran four or five pounds in Sebago. Or perhaps a togue—a lake trout—which might be even bigger, and which ventured toward the surface only during the first week or two after ice-out.

Mostly, though, I remember long, cold, rainy April days on the water in a leaky rowboat with my father. His attention never seemed to wander. When I got restless, he told me stories, and I understood that if you already had a storehouse full of fishing memories, it was easy to pay attention.

"Try twiggling," he'd tell me. "Give it some action." And he'd pick up his rod and saw it back and forth awhile, and although I don't remember ever having a salmon strike when I was holding my rod in my hands, I never doubted the magical properties of twiggling.

It's been many years since my father and I trolled streamers for landlocked salmon on Sebago Lake. Now, he says, it's time I took my son to Sebago. Every boy, says Dad, should know what it's like to have his tip dip and his rod bounce and his reel screech and to see a wild, silvery arc explode from the gray, wind-chopped surface of a big Maine lake.

We're going to do it. I know that on a cold, rainswept April day, dragging a Gray Ghost and a Dark Edson Tiger tandem off the stern of an old rowboat will still work. If my son's attention wanders, as it will, of course, I'll tell him stories from my own storehouse of memories—how old Charley Watkins called every spring to herald the opening of a new fishing season, how Tom Craven and Gorham Cross and the Putnam brothers, my father's friends, shared their cabin and their stories with me, how they fished all day, then cooked steak and eggs at the woodstove and snored all night.

When the fishing gets slow, I'll show my boy how to twiggle. These are the important things that a father must pass to his son.

How to Turn a Perfectly Normal Child into a Fisherman

From *Pavlov's Trout*

PAUL QUINNETT

Several years ago I was consulted by a highly agitated mother who felt something dreadful was happening to her son.

"A fatal disease?" I asked.

"It's worse. At least they're working on cures for fatal diseases."

"What then?"

"He wants to become a fishing guide."

Sometimes in an interview psychologists are required to put in extra effort to keep a straight fa— . . . , uh, maintain our decorum.

I realized that, given my lust for angling and the risk that admitting this might have on a potential client, my next question had to be purged of any interviewer bias or excess emotion and delivered in the most impartial, professional voice possible.

walleye

"Walleye or salmon?" I queried.

The woman gave me one of those long, penetrating stares clients reserve for the moment when they have confirmed their worst fear, that shrinks need shrinks.

Realizing she'd seen through my professional façade, I acknowledged my prejudice toward fishing and offered to refer her to someone who played golf.

"Oh my God, no!" she cried. "My ex-husband played golf. But since you're a fisherman, maybe you can tell me why they're all so crazy."

I didn't take offense at the question.

In a matter of minutes, I had explained that fishermen were no worse than most sportsmen of passion, and considerably better off than many.

"How?" she queried.

"Well, they tend to be happier, more contented, and less stressed."

"They sound like milk cows," she mused. "But, what about my son? He's obsessed with fishing and thinks of nothing else."

I smiled. "He may have a case of the passions."

"The 'passions'?"

"It's a kind of magnificent obsession with angling," I explained dreamily. "You see, fishing is always rewarding, always satisfying, always challenging, always . . ."

"Just a minute," interrupted the lady. "You sound as crazy as my son. And he gets that same stupid glint in his eye that I see in yours. I tell you I'm worried. He's nineteen and should be in college. What do I do?"

Clients are always asking tough questions like this. For some reason, they want quick solutions to knotty problems. Fortunately, we psychologists are highly trained in dodging obvious queries. If you give advice and it works, you get the credit while the client becomes dependent and doesn't grow. If you give advice and it *doesn't work*, you come off looking stupid beyond belief. If things really go sour, you might get sued. Therefore, the answer to all requests for advice is to ask the same question you were just asked.

"What do you think you should do?" I asked.

"I don't know," said the woman. "Say . . . what is this? If I could get him to do what I want him to do I wouldn't be in here seeing you."

Another thing they teach in graduate school is how to handle frustrated and angry clients.

Once I explained to the woman I had always wanted to be a fishing guide myself, and that there was no way I could objectively consult her on how she might handle her son's request to spend his college savings on a twenty-foot jet boat, she accepted my referral to a nonfishing colleague and we terminated any professional relationship. Of course, I asked if she had one of her son's business cards, and I didn't charge her for the session.

Several years later I ran into this woman in a department store. She lost the battle with her son and he guided for a couple of years in Alaska before returning to the Lower 48 and starting college. Unless I miss my guess, he did not major in psychology.

Raising Fishermen

Fishermen seem to spring up in nonfishing families with some regularity, as in the case I just described, but more often the child is aimed at the fishing life by its mother and father. Bull's-eyes are not guaranteed.

Though no one has ever asked me, I have always wanted to tell parents how to raise fishermen. As a father of three and consultant to many, I know about the vulnerabilities of little minds and, therefore, how to implant the sport of angling deep into the psychological core of an otherwise innocent child. As a one-time college instructor in developmental psychology, I am prepared to offer my own formula for rearing anglers. This formula also works to inoculate children against drug abuse and install self-esteem, subjects that will be further explained in the chapter on fishaholism.

Nature vs. Nurture

Are fishermen born to the sport or do they acquire the habit? Down through the centuries, people have pondered this and similar questions regarding great generals, opera singers, world-class athletes, and theoretical physicists.

Dr. John B. Watson, the famous behavioral psychologist and learning theorist, once said if given enough time and total control of the environment, he could turn any given baby into a doctor, lawyer, or Indian chief.

Can you start with any old baby and turn it into a happy, contented, clear-eyed adult with a love of angling? Sure you can. The research says so. Down through the years Dr. Watson has been proved more right than wrong. Except for some hard-core personality traits and the limitations of genetically determined things like height and eye color, nurture wins.

There is no known antifishing gene. If anything, there is probably a pro-fishing gene, so raising fishermen should be no more difficult than raising Democrats. In the bargain, you can end up with an ethical sportsman who loves and respects nature and holds ecologically sound conservation values that last a lifetime.

What more, I ask any parent, could you possibly want?

Start Early

You cannot begin your project too soon. Consider, for example, this fictionalized announcement from the *New York Times*:

"Born to Mr. and Mrs. Wendall P. Terry, an eight-pound, two-ounce fisherman. The baby angler was deftly netted by Dr. T. S. Morgan, himself a fly fisherman and longtime member of Trout Unlimited. The baby will be christened Lee Wulff Terry, after the world-famous fisherman of the same name."

There is great power in naming. In ancient times, names were so special they had to be given to you under extraordinary circumstances. Your name could come to you in a dream, or be given you by an elder, but in any event, it was your name and only suited you. It set the course for your life.

Announcing the birth of a fisherman with a strong fishing name, in hopes of casting the die after nine months of pregnancy, though, is probably too late. To get a neonate headed in the right direction, you can actually begin well before the fetus is fully developed.

We know from several research studies that a little one is quite capable of learning while still in the oven. A fetus exposed to pieces by Beethoven while in the womb will, several years later, learn to play those same pieces more quickly than others, providing evidence human learning takes place in the womb. I used to tell my classes this old story about an Englishwoman to drive this prebirth learning point home.

There was once a recently impregnated woman who very much wanted her child to be both a fisherman and well mannered. To get the desired result, the lady read books on manners and stream etiquette to her swelling abdomen for the entire nine months of her pregnancy.

The nine months passed, but no child came. Then ten months. Then a year. Then two years and still no child. At the five-year mark, the lady was huge and quite uncomfortable, but there were still no signs of labor. A decade passed. Then two decades. After some thirty-five years, the lady passed away.

When the medical examiner opened her up, he found two fully grown English fishermen engaged in the following conversation:

"No, *you* go first."

"No, you. I insist. This is your beat."

"I'm very sorry, sir, but I believe it is your beat and, therefore, you should exit and take the first cast."

"Quite the contrary, my dear man. But thank you, anyway. Now, please, be a good sport, take your leave, and make the first cast."

This absolutely true story suggests several important steps that can be taken by couples hoping to raise an angler.

First, try to conceive the child during a fishing trip. I have no research to document the importance of environmental settings and their influence on matters of conception and eventual outcomes, but how could it hurt?

Next, because positive in-utero influences have salutary effects, I cannot see the harm in the following prescriptions:

Expose the fisherman-in-progress to the sounds of water; babbling brooks, pounding surf, waves lapping against canoe sides, etc.

Exposures to the sound of a screaming reel, shouts of "One

on!" and the general sort of fishing chatter that accrues during a day on the water might give the tyke a leg up on angling jargon later on.

The mother-to-be should probably eat a lot of fish during the pregnancy.

Research has shown that both fetuses and infants are relaxed by the gentle swaying of the mother. What could better ready a child for a fishing future than easy hikes to remote lakes, the rocking motion of a boat, and the rhythmic action of Mom while she whips a fly rod back and forth, back and forth while whispering of rising trout, caddis hatches, and humming those joyful little tunes that sometimes bubble up from the heart during moments of great pleasure.

Both Mom and Dad might read fishing poems and stories to the swelling belly. As long as twins are not expected and you lay off the etiquette, what possible risks could there be?

Get the Birth Myth Right

All of us have a birth myth. Sometimes the myth is given to us, sometimes we make up our own. For example, if three guys in long beards are guided by a supernova to your mother's delivery room and happen to bring along some incense and myrrh, you're likely to grow up with a lot of people expecting you to do big things.

On the other hand, if you're in a quarrel with your parents about something and think they don't love you anymore, you may create your own birth myth. "There was a mixup at the hospital. I'm someone else's kid." Or, "I must have been adopted."

A fisherman's birth myth might include being born on the opening day of walleye season, or at the height of the green drake hatch, or in the back of a bass boat. Being named "Izaak" after Izaak Walton or "Lee" after Lee Wulff also fits the bill.

Alexander the Great's birth myth was that he would conquer the world. This expectation was laid on him by his folks, some Macedonian soothsayers, and the fact of his royal birth, and after a little trouble in Asia Minor, he did conquer what he knew of the planet. Whether kings, conquerors, or casting champions, the process works the same. The important thing to remember is that parents have a great deal to do with what sort of myth the kid grows up with, and therefore, his destiny.

The birth myth the fisherman father hands to his offspring will typically include a number of psychological expectations, including the imagined warm companionship that will begin once the child is old enough to become "my little fishin' buddy."

This leads me to an observation about where the trouble begins for half of our population.

How many fathers look at a brand-spanking-new baby girl and think "fishin' buddy"? Not enough, I can tell you. More parents put a damper on things by seeing fishing as a "boy thing" or referring to worms as "icky." If you don't think of girls as fishers from the very start, the odds are heavily stacked against any little girl growing up to love the sport. Almost all the avid fisherwomen I know were brought to the sport by their fathers.

As we expect of children, so shall they grow.

If you want a daughter to grow up to fish with you, give her a fitting birth myth. If it's true, tell her she was born the day the first salmon returned to the river, the day the big pike was caught, or the morning the ice went out of the bay and the lake trout began to hit. Anything. Use visualization to set the goal.

If you're a trouter, close your eyes and "see" her standing side by side with you, knee-deep in your favorite stream. See a rod in her hand. See her dressed in hip boots, a light green vest, and a yellow fishing hat with matching trim. See a smile on her bright little face. Now see that smile widen to a great grin as a nice rainbow rises to take her fly. To get what you want, follow Thoreau's advice, "Print your hopes upon your mind."

Setting Up the Classroom

With a fishing birth myth in place, the next question is "How old should my child be before exposing her to angling?"

Very recent research on newborns indicates that, while we once thought they had poor and blurry vision in the first weeks of life, they actually see perfectly at a distance of nine inches. This is the approximate distance from the mother's breast to her face, and therefore the recommended distance for early exposure to fish pictures and fishing videos.

I'm speaking here of what psychologists call an "enriched environment." While a lot of research has been done on the possible beneficial effects of enriched stimulation, the results do not strongly support the idea that an especially busy, stimulating, enriched environment actually leads to things like higher IQ. But then again, there are no data to suggest it hurts.

Early exposure certainly won't hurt. Of all the nursery rhymes my mother read me, this excerpt from one by Eugene Field most helped cast the die:

> Wynken, Blynken, and Nod one night
> Sailed off in a wooden shoe;
> Sailed on a river of crystal light
> Into a sea of dew.
>
> "Where are you going, and what do you wish?"
> The old moon asked of the three.
> "We have come to fish for the herring fish
> That live in this beautiful sea.
> Nets of silver and gold have we,"
> Said Wynken, Blynken, and Nod.
>
> The old moon laughed and sang a song
> As they rocked in the wooden shoe,
> And the wind that sped them all night long
> Ruffled the waves of dew.

The little stars were the herring fish
That lived in that beautiful sea.
"Now cast your nets wherever you wish;
Never afeared are we!"
So cried the stars to the fishermen three:
Wynken, Blynken, and Nod.

"How old should my child be before I take her fishing?"

My advice is to wait until the child is safely out of diapers, but not so long that it has learned to sass. I started taking some of my children with me when they were but two and three years of age. If you wait until they are speaking in complete sentences you may have missed a critical learning window.

The "when" question is best answered by what I call the "set up." If you set up a first fishing experience properly, the child will have little choice but to love the sport, and here's the set up:

Only take the child with you when the weather is good. There is no point in ruining a kid by freezing her solid her first time out.

Plan to return home in no more than three hours, well before any signs of crankiness or fatigue develop. The younger the child, the shorter the attention span and, therefore, the shorter the first fishing trip.

Unfinished business tends to be remembered best psychologically. It's better to exit a hot bite and leave the little rascal with the notion that the fish are always there, always hungry, and waiting for her return. She'll dream fishing dreams between trips and pester you to take her again.

Be sure the first fishing trip has a high probability of success. Bluegill, crappie, or put-and-take trout ponds, including commercial ones, will get the job done. What you don't want is a kid to get blanked and bored.

Don't buy all her tackle before you go. Once she's hooked, she'll start hinting around for gear. I know of no better way to keep a child's room clean or the lawn mowed than trading fishing tackle for chores.

"Will my child enjoy fishing?" I wouldn't worry too much about it. The fish take care of the excitement requirements. All you have to do is take the time and make the setting as pleasant as possible. As long as a fishing trip doesn't become a time to discipline a child or work on some problem or other, the companionship, shared affection, and fun provided by the finny ones will take care of any pleasure-principle business.

Observational Learning

The most powerful way to teach a child about fishing takes place without the teacher trying. Observational learning, which I wrote my doctorial dissertation on, is the process by which humans observe and imitate one another to acquire everything from attitudes to casting techniques. All of us learn by imitating, as any parent who hears his two-year-old suddenly say "dammit anyway" can tell you.

Kids learn to repeat exactly what they see . . . and hear. If you operate on the "Do as I say, not as I do" model, your little imitators will copy exactly what you say and do, thus becoming little hypocrites themselves. Things like racial prejudice, bigotry, and greed are learned well before age five. So are things like fishing manners and catch-and-release.

Your mother taught you to watch the hostess if you're caught at a fancy dinner party with too much silver lined up around your plate. A child learns by watching which bass plug his father selects for a lily-pad situation. Every adult is a potential model for every child, and the closer the relationship between the model and the child, the more powerful will be the influence. Taking a kid fishing is a great responsibility and a great opportunity.

By observing and imitating, little fishermen learn life's most critical lessons: parenting skills, sex roles, problem-solving strategies, ethics, and how to unhook and release a trout without hurting it. If you stop for a moment to think about how humans are first socialized and brought into the family of man, you will realize observational learning is the key. Without learning by watching, none of us would get very far.

Before the advent of the modern family, children were never very far from their parents, or aunts or uncles or grandfathers. As soon as a boy could toss a fishing spear, he was given one. If an old man was going down to the stream to seine a batch of fish for supper, the children tagged along. Natural settings were the classrooms of fishermen past. They worked perfectly then, and they can work perfectly today, but *you have to take the kid fishing with you.*

Observational learning is fast and powerful. If you're a reasonably calm and likable person without too many bad habits like swearing in front of children when you break off a lunker, you don't need to do anything special to teach a child all the important lessons about becoming a fisherman, but you can't teach a child to fish by telling fishing stories. You must take the kid fishing. And since I highly approve of enlightened self-interest in parent models, you should take the little imitator fishing as often as you possibly can. If you don't have someone of your own, take someone else's little boy or girl.

Long ago and far away I was laboring diligently on my Ph.D. in a quiet alcove of a university library when one of those dark, doubt-shrouded questions suddenly grabbed me by the scruff of the neck and threw me to the floor.

"Who," the spook demanded, "do you think gives a damn what 'ontogeny recapitulates phylogeny' really means? Believe me, no one will ever ask. Why are you wasting your life memorizing nonsense like this when you could be out bass fishing!?"

It was a warm afternoon in May when the spook jumped me in that musty old library. The smallmouth were hitting like crazy not twenty miles away down on the Snake River.

I had a big exam in child development the next day and my reputation as an academician was on the line. The existential struggle over what to do was exquisite. But I pulled through. I caught a half dozen nice smallies before nightfall.

I took my oldest boy fishing with me that day. By doing so, I may have inadvertently modeled something truly important for him, that while there will always be one more exam in this life, there may never be another perfect May afternoon to take a child fishing.

My wife, Ann, held the best counsel during the years she mostly raised our children while I was stuck in some class or behind the stacks at the university library. Aware of the risks inherent in earning a higher education at the cost of common sense, she always knew exactly what to do when I came home spiking some high academic fever or other and hot for some experiment on the kids.

"Hands off," she would say. "These are your children, not lab animals. No home experiments. Just take them fishing. You can't foul them up too much if you just take them fishing."

She was, as usual, dead right.

Fishing with My Father

PERIE LONGO

In memory of Dale Hartley Adams

July 6, 1913–June 20, 1991

He always took me fishing with him
on those long northern summer nights
out in the boat and I loved it, not the sitting for hours
under all the moons and showy red lights, but the going—
the creak of the oars in the locks like entering
an attic of silence where no one could reach us,
water beads lined up on the edge of the oar
clinging like a string of pearls before they dripped back
into the liquid mirror that held us all. I realize now
how many poems I thought up but never noted
in those hours while we stared the bobber down
praying for a catch. I used to play games to pass the time,
for it was not the fishing that pleased me

but being with my father
in his joy. If I blinked my eyes thirty-nine times,
on the fortieth a muskie would strike, that fish
my father's dream he took to heaven, I think.
When I held his arm at his passing,
clung to his hand like no fish ever had,
he let go and I slipped off, like that.
If I blink thirty-nine times, on the fortieth
maybe I'll catch a glimpse of him.

From *A River Runs Through It*

Norman Maclean

I didn't catch one right away, and I didn't expect to. My side of the river was the quiet water, the right side to be on in the hole above where the stone flies were hatching, but the drowned stone flies were washed down in the powerful water on the other side of this hole. After seven or eight casts, though, a small ring appeared on the surface. A small ring usually means that a small fish has risen to the surface, but it can also mean a big fish has rolled under water. If it is a big fish under water, he won't look so much like a fish as an arch of a rainbow that has appeared and disappeared.

Paul didn't even wait to see if I landed him. He waded out to talk to me. He went on talking as if I had time to listen to him and land a big fish. He said, "I'm going to wade back again and fish the rest of the hole." Sometimes I said, "Yes," and when the fish went out of the water, speech failed me, and when the fish made a long run I said at the end of it, "You'll have to say that over again."

Finally, we understood each other. He was going to wade the river again and fish the other side. We both should fish fairly fast, because Father probably was already waiting for us. Paul threw his cigarette in the water and was gone without seeing whether I landed the fish.

Not only was I on the wrong side of the river to fish with drowned stone flies, but Paul was a good enough roll caster to have already fished most of my side from his own. But I caught two more. They also started as little circles that looked like little fish feeding on the surface but were broken arches of big rainbows under water. After I caught these two, I quit. They made ten, and the last three were the finest fish I ever caught. They weren't the biggest or most spectacular fish I ever caught, but they were three fish I caught because my brother waded across the river to give me the fly that would catch them and because they were the last fish I ever caught fishing with him.

After cleaning my fish, I set these three apart with a layer of grass and wild mint.

Then I lifted the heavy basket, shook myself into the shoulder strap until it didn't cut any more, and thought, "I'm through for the day. I'll go down and sit on the bank by my father and talk." Then I added, "If he doesn't feel like talking, I'll just sit."

I could see the sun ahead. The coming burst of light made it look from the shadows that I and a river inside the earth were about to appear on earth. Although I could as yet see only the sunlight and not anything in it, I knew my father was sitting somewhere on the bank. I knew partly because he and I shared many of the same impulses, even to quitting at about the same time. I was sure without as yet being able to see into what was in front of me that he was sitting somewhere in the sunshine reading the New Testament in Greek. I knew this both from instinct and experience.

Old age had brought him moments of complete peace. Even when we went duck hunting and the roar of the early morning shooting was over, he would sit in the blind wrapped in an old army blanket with his Greek New Testament in one hand and his shotgun in the other. When a stray duck happened by, he would drop the book and raise the gun, and, after the shooting was over, he would raise the book again, occasionally interrupting his reading to thank his dog for retrieving the duck.

The voices of the subterranean river in the shadows were different from the voices of the sunlit river ahead. In the shadows against the cliff the river was deep and engaged in profundities, circling back on itself now and then to say things over to be sure it had understood itself. But the river ahead came out into the sunny world like a chatterbox, doing its best to be friendly. It bowed to one shore and then to the other so nothing would feel neglected.

By now I could see inside the sunshine and had located my father. He was sitting high on the bank. He wore no hat. Inside the sunlight, his faded red hair was once again ablaze and again in glory. He was reading, although evidently only by sentences because he often looked away from the book. He did not close the book until some time after he saw me.

I scrambled up the bank and asked him, "How many did you get?" He said, "I got four or five." I asked, "Are they any good?" He said, "They are beautiful."

He was about the only man I ever knew who used the word "beautiful" as a natural form of speech, and I guess I picked up the habit from hanging around him when I was little.

"How many did you catch?" he asked. "I also caught all I want," I told him. He omitted asking me just how many that was, but he did ask me, "Are they any good?" "They are beautiful," I told him, and sat down beside him.

"What have you been reading?" I asked. "A book," he said. It was on the ground on the other side of him. So I would not have to bother to look over his knees to see it, he said, "A good book."

Then he told me, "In the part I was reading it says the Word was in the beginning, and that's right. I used to think water was first, but if you listen carefully you will hear that the words are underneath the water."

"That's because you are a preacher first and then a fisherman," I told him. "If you ask Paul, he will tell you that the words are formed out of water."

"No," my father said, "you are not listening carefully. The water runs over the words. Paul will tell you the same thing. Where is Paul anyway?"

I told him he had gone back to fish the first hole over again. "But he promised to be here soon," I assured him. "He'll be here when he catches his limit," he said. "He'll be here soon," I reassured him, partly because I could already see him in the subterranean shadows.

My father went back to reading and I tried to check what we had said by listening. Paul was fishing fast, picking up one here and there and wasting no time in walking them to shore. When he got directly across from us, he held up a finger on each hand and my father said, "He needs two more for his limit."

I looked to see where the book was left open and knew just enough Greek to recognize λόγς as the Word. I guessed from it and the argument that I was looking at the first verse of John. While I was looking, Father said, "He has one on."

It was hard to believe, because he was fishing in front of us on the other side of the hole that Father had just fished. Father slowly rose, found a good-sized rock and held it behind his back. Paul landed the fish, and waded out again for number twenty and his limit. Just as he was making the first cast, Father threw the rock. He was old enough so that he threw awkwardly and afterward had to rub his shoulder, but the rock landed in the river about where Paul's fly landed and at about the same time, so you can see where my brother learned to throw rocks into his partner's fishing water when he couldn't bear to see his partner catch any more fish.

Paul was startled for only a moment. Then he spotted Father on the bank rubbing his shoulder, and Paul laughed, shook his fist at him, backed to shore and went downstream until he was out of rock range. From there he waded into the water and began to cast again, but now he was far enough away so we couldn't see his line or loops. He was a man with a wand in a river, and whatever happened we had to guess from what the man and the wand and the river did.

As he waded out, his big right arm swung back and forth. Each circle of his arm inflated his chest. Each circle was faster and higher and longer until his arm became defiant and his chest breasted the sky. On shore we were sure, although we could see no line, that the air above him was singing with loops of line that never touched the water but got bigger and bigger each time they passed and sang. And we knew what was in his mind from the lengthening defiance of his arm. He was not going to let his fly touch any water close to shore where the small and middle-sized fish were. We knew from his arm and chest that all parts of him were saying, "No small one for the last one." Everything was going into one big cast for one last big fish.

From our angle high on the bank, my father and I could see where in the distance the wand was going to let the fly first touch water. In the middle of the river was a rock iceberg, just its tip exposed above water and underneath it a rock house.

It met all the residential requirements for big fish—powerful water carrying food to the front and back doors, and rest and shade behind them.

My father said, "There has to be a big one out there."

I said, "A little one couldn't live out there."

My father said, "The big one wouldn't let it."

My father could tell by the width of Paul's chest that he was going to let the next loop sail. It couldn't get any wider. "I wanted to fish out there," he said, "but I couldn't cast that far."

Paul's body pivoted as if he were going to drive a gold ball three hundred yards, and his arm went high into the great arc and the tip of his wand bent like a spring, and then everything sprang and sang.

Suddenly, there was an end of action. The man was immobile. There was no bend, no power in the wand. It pointed at ten o'clock and ten o'clock pointed at the rock. For a moment the man looked like a teacher with a pointer illustrating something about a rock to a rock. Only water moved. Somewhere above the top of the rock house a fly was swept in water so powerful only a big fish could be there to see it.

Then the universe stepped on its third rail. The wand jumped convulsively as it made contact with the magic current of the world. The wand tried to jump out of the man's right hand. His left hand seemed to be frantically waving good-bye to a fish, but actually was trying to throw enough line into the rod to reduce the voltage and ease the shock of what had struck.

Everything seemed electrically charged but electrically

unconnected. Electrical sparks appeared here and there on the river. A fish jumped so far downstream that it seemed outside the man's electrical field, but, when the fish had jumped, the man had leaned back on the rod and it was then that the fish had toppled back into the water not guided in its reentry by itself. The connections between the convulsions and the sparks became clearer by repetition. When the man leaned back on the wand and the fish reentered the water not altogether under its own power, the wand recharged with convulsions, the man's hand waved frantically at another departure, and much farther below a fish jumped again. Because of the connections, it became the same fish.

The fish made three such long runs before another act in the performance began. Although the act involved a big man and a big fish, it looked more like children playing. The man's left hand sneakily began recapturing line, and then, as if caught in the act, threw it all back into the rod as the fish got wise and made still another run.

"He'll get him," I assured my father.

"Beyond doubt," my father said. The line going out became shorter than what the left hand took in.

When Paul peered into the water behind him, we knew he was going to start working the fish to shore and didn't want to back into a hole or rock. We could tell he had worked the fish into shallow water because he held the rod higher and higher to keep the fish from bumping into anything on the bottom. Just when we thought the performance was over, the wand convulsed and the man thrashed through the water after some unseen power departing for the deep.

"The son of a bitch still has fight in him," I thought I said to myself, but unmistakably I said it out loud, and was embarrassed for having said it out loud in front of my father. He said nothing.

Two or three more times Paul worked him close to shore, only to have him swirl and return to the deep, but even at that distance my father and I could feel the ebbing of the underwater power. The rod went high in the air, and the man moved backwards swiftly but evenly, motions which when translated into events meant the fish had tried to rest for a moment on top of the water and the man had quickly raised the rod high and skidded him to shore before the fish thought of getting under water again. He skidded him across the rocks clear back to a sandbar before the shocked fish gasped and discovered he could not live in oxygen. In belated despair, he rose in the sand and consumed the rest of momentary life dancing the Dance of Death on his tail.

The man put the wand down, got on his hands and knees in the sand, and, like an animal, circled another animal and waited. Then the shoulder shot straight out, and my brother stood up, faced us, and, with uplifted arm proclaimed himself the victor. Something giant dangled from his fist. Had Romans been watching they would have thought that what was dangling had a helmet on it.

"That's his limit," I said to my father.

"He is beautiful," my father said, although my brother had just finished catching his limit in the hole my father had already fished.

This was the last fish we were ever to see Paul catch. My father and I talked about this moment several times later, and whatever our other feelings, we always felt it fitting that, when we saw him catch his last fish, we never saw the fish but only the artistry of the fisherman.

While my father was watching my brother, he reached over to pat me, but he missed, so he had to turn his eyes and look for my knee and try again. He must have thought that I felt neglected and that he should tell me he was proud of me also but for other reasons.

It was a little too deep and fast where Paul was trying to wade the river, and he knew it. He was crouched over the water and his arms were spread wide for balance. If you were a wader of big rivers you could have felt with him even at a distance the power of the water making his legs weak and wavy and ready to swim out from under him. He looked downstream to estimate how far it was to an easier place to wade.

My father said, "He won't take the trouble to walk downstream. He'll swim it." At the same time Paul thought the same thing, and put his cigarettes and matches in his hat.

My father and I sat on the bank and laughed at each other. It never occurred to either of us to hurry to the shore in case he needed help with a rod in his right hand and a basket loaded with fish on his left shoulder. In our family it was no great thing for a fisherman to swim a river with matches in his hair. We laughed at each other because we knew he was getting damn good and wet, and we lived in him, and were swept over the rocks with him and held his rod high in one of our hands.

As he moved to shore he caught himself on his feet and then was washed off them, and, when he stood again, more of him showed and he staggered to shore. He never stopped to shake himself. He came charging up the bank showering molecules of water and images of himself to show what was sticking out of his basket, and he dripped all over us, like a young duck dog that in its joy forgets to shake itself before getting close.

"Let's put them all out on the grass and take a picture of them," he said. So we emptied our baskets and arranged them by size and took turns photographing each other admiring them and ourselves. The photographs turned out to be like most amateur snapshots of fishing catches—the fish were white from overexposure and didn't look as big as they actually were and the fishermen looked self-conscious as if some guide had to catch the fish for them.

However, one closeup picture of him at the end of this day remains in my mind, as if fixed by some chemical bath. Usually, just after he finished fishing he had little to say unless he saw he could have fished better. Otherwise, he merely smiled. Now flies danced around his hatband. Large drops of water ran from under his hat onto his face and then into his lips when he smiled.

At the end of this day, then, I remember him both as a distant abstraction in artistry and a closeup in water and laughter.

My father always felt shy when compelled to praise one of his family, and his family always felt shy when he praised them. My father said, "You are a fine fisherman."

My brother said, "I'm pretty good with a rod, but I need three more years before I can think like a fish."

Remembering that he had caught his limit by switching to George's No. 2 Yellow Hackle with a feather wing, I said without knowing how much I said, "You already know how to think like a dead stone fly."

We sat on the bank and the river went by. As always, it was making sounds to itself, and now it made sounds to us. It would be hard to find three men sitting side by side who knew better what a river was saying.

Sons

From *The Longest Silence*

Thomas McGuane

Both my parents were Irish Catholics from Massachusetts.
My father had had enough of the Harp Way and was glad
to get out of there and move to Michigan. My mother never
accepted it and would have been happy to raise a nest of Micks
anywhere between Boston and New Bedford. Every summer
she did the next-best thing and packed us children up and
took us "home" to Fall River. My father seemed glad to watch
us go. I still see him in our driveway with the parakeet in its
cage, trying unsuccessfully to get my mother to take the bird
too so he wouldn't even have to hang around long enough to
feed it. At the end of the summer, when we returned from
Massachusetts, the bird would be perched in there but it was
never the same bird. It was another $3.95 blue parakeet but
without the gentleness of our old bird. When we reached into
the cage to get our friend, we usually got bitten.

We traveled on one of the wonderful lake boats that crossed Lake Erie to Buffalo, and I remember the broad interior staircases and the brassbound window through which one contemplated the terrific paddlewheels. I hoped intensely that a fish would be swept up from deep in the lake and brought to my view but it never happened. Then we took the train, I guess it must've been to Boston. I mostly recall my rapture as we swept through the eastern countryside over brooks and rivers that I knew were the watery world of the fish and turtles I cared so madly about. One of these trips must have been made during hard times, because my mother emphasized that there was only enough money for us children to eat; and it is true that we had wild highs and lows as my father tried to build a business.

Many wonderful things happened during my endless summers with my grandmother, aunts, and uncles in Fall River, but for present purposes, I am thinking only of fishing. Those original images are still so burning that I struggle to find a proper syntax for them. In the first, my father arrived and took me up to see some shirttail cousins up in Townsend. A little brook passed through their backyard and, lying on my stomach, I could look into one of its pools and see tiny brook trout swimming. It was something close to the ecstasy I felt when I

brook trout

held my ear against the slots of the toaster and heard a supernal music from heaven ringing through the toaster springs. The brook trout were water angels and part of the first America, the one owned by the Indians, whose music I'd listened to in the toaster. I had seen the old Indian trails, their burial mounds and the graves of settlers killed in the French and Indian wars. For some reason I knew King Philip—or Metacomet, as the Indians called him—had eaten them.

All this seemed to be part of a lost world, like the world I was losing as my father became more absorbed in his work. We had good times together only when fish were present, and those brook trout are the first memories. It was casually easy for us to get along fishing; the rest was a bomb. I think of the fathers-and-sons day at his athletic club with particular loathing, as it was an annual ordeal. Silver dollars were hurled into the swimming pool for the boys to vie for. Each father stood by the pool, gazing at the writhing young divers and waiting for his silver-laden son to surface. Rarely coming up with a coin, I was conscious of appearing to be less than an altogether hale boy and hardly worth bringing to this generational fete, with its ventriloquists and Irish tenors or more usually, the maniacal Eddie Peabody on the banjo. All of this was an aspect of the big dust we were meant to make in our mid-American boom town where sport of the most refined sort quickly sank into alcoholic mayhem. Steaks in the backyard, pill-popping housewives, and golf were the order of the day, and many youngsters sought to get their fathers away somewhere in search of a fish. Most of our fathers were just off the farm or out of small towns and heading vertically upward into a new world. We didn't want them to go and we didn't want to go with them.

I thought that if I devised a way to free my father from his rigorous job, we could fish more. I saw an ad for a Hart, Shaffner and Marx suit that said it was for the man who wanted to look like he would make ten thousand a year before he was thirty. (Remember, this was many years ago.) I told my father that he ought to make ten thousand a year, then ten thousand a year in eleven months, then ten thousand a year in ten months and so on, and with this properly earned free time, he and I would go fishing together more often. "With an attitude like that," my father boomed, "you'd never make ten thousand a year in the first place."

None of this mattered in Massachusetts. Across Brownell Street from my grandmother, between Main and Almy, lived Jimmy McDermott, an elegant Irish bachelor and his spinster sister, Alice. They seemed very sophisticated and witty, especially compared to their immediate neighbors, the Sullivans, who were unreconstructed Irish, with a scowling mother in a black shawl and an impenetrable brogue. Jimmy McDermott took me fishing and bought me my first reel, a beautiful Penn Senator surf-casting reel whose black density seemed to weigh coolly in my hands. Jimmy McDermott detected that I needed someone to take me fishing.

He thought it was crazy for a boy who loved to fish to be

hanging around Brownell Street in Fall River in August, so he packed a lunch and we went fishing for tautog along some small and lonely beach with its granite outcroppings and sun-shot salty fog and tidal aromas. We caught several fish on the fierce green crabs we used for bait and I heard about several more, because Jimmy was the sort of person who made sure at such a sacramental moment as angling that the full timbre of the thing must be appreciated by the recounting of such holy incidents in time, of striped bass and flounders, the gloomy conger eel who filled three skillets with grease or the rich sports in the old days who baited their bass rigs with small lobsters. A Portuguese family picnicked on the nearby strand, and in my somewhat more global view today I think of us amusing ourselves on that *mare nostrum*, the Atlantic Ocean, casting our hopes on those ancestral waters toward Ireland, the Azores, toward the Old World. The sea heaved up around our rocks, pulling a white train of foam from mid-ocean along with its mysteries of distance and language, drownings, cara-vels, unwitnessed thousand-foot thunderheads, phosphorous and fish by the square mile.

It is a great triumph over something—biology, maybe, or whatever part of modern history has prolonged adolescence to the threshold of senility—for a father to view his son without skepticism. I have not quite achieved this state but at least have identified the problem. Therefore, when I stood at the airport in Cancún and watched my frequently carefree son emerge with several disintegrating carry-on bags and his shirt hanging out of his pants, I did not take this altogether as a sign of complete disorganization.

When we hugged, because he's so much stronger, he rather knocked the wind out of me. And when we made our way to the small aircraft that would take us to Ascension Bay, I asked if he had practiced his casting. "Once," he said.

"These aren't trout," I said. "A thirty-foot cast doesn't get it."

"Don't worry about it," he smiled. "I don't expect to have any problem with bonefish."

"How can you say that?" I asked. "You've never seen one before, you don't know how tough they can be." He smiled again, knowing exactly how to drive me crazy.

We had a comfortable, really wonderful cottage with cool concrete walls and a roof of thatched monkey palm. Birds were everywhere and the blue Caribbean breakers rose high enough that you could look right through them, then fell. Just past the line of breakers, the coral garden seemed like a submerged quilt.

Thomas was slow in getting ready to fish. He was bent over the sink, doing something and taking too long about it. I said we ought to hurry up and head for the boat. I said it twice and he straightened up from the sink holding a pale green scorpion he had just extracted from the drain. "In case you were thinking of brushing your teeth," he said, and grabbed his rod.

Our guide was a Maya Indian named Pedro, a solid fifty-year-old of easygoing authority. I thought of a Little Compton voice of yesteryear—"We've been here for generations"—Pedro's family had been on the shores of this bay since thousands of years before Christ. As Pedro was a mildly intolerant man, all business, one soon learned not to pester him with trifles. I did ask if he had ever visited the United States.

"I've never been to Mexico," he said coolly.

Walking to the boat, I was excited to see a lineated woodpecker who loves to eat Aztec ants from their home in the hollow pumpwood tree. A brave soul, he defends his nest against toucans. Ruddy ground doves scattered along our trail and we saw the splendid chacalaca on the edge of the jungle, noisy as a chicken in flight. When we set out in the skiff, mangrove swallows scattered across the narrow channels. My son explained to me that some birds had taken to flying upside down over New York City because "there was nothing worth shitting on." Birds have much to tell us.

Pedro ran the skiff through the shallow water wilderness with the air he seemed to bring to everything, an absence of ambiguity. There was no scanning the horizon or searching for signs. If a tremulous ridge of tidal movement betrayed a shoal in our path, Pedro adjusted his angle of travel without ever looking in the direction of the hazard.

When we emerged completely from the congestion of cays, remarkably similar bands of pale blue, of sky and sea, stretched before us at a sublime scale, white tropical clouds reaching upward to heavenly elevations. A scattering of small islands lay in the distance.

I was still thinking of Pedro's answer about never having been to Mexico. Quintana Roo was his country. In my minimal Spanish, I decided to pose a peculiar question. "Pedro, to us this is an extraordinary place, a beautiful place. But you have never been anywhere else. My question is this: Do you realize and appreciate that you live in one of the world's great places?" He pulled his head back and, pursing his lips to state the obvious, said in an impassioned growl, "*Sí, señor!*"

Thomas was in the bow of the boat, line stripped out, and Pedro was poling along a muddy bank near the mangroves. A squadron of bonefish had come out of the light, our blind side, and flushed in a starburst of wakes. It wasn't really a shot, so Thomas remained in the bow, ready. After a while, I felt Pedro kick the stem of the bow out to position him and declare, "*macabi*"—bonefish—in his quiet but insistent way that made it clear he expected no screw-ups. We stared hard, testing Pedro's patience, then made out the bonefish about seventy feet away. He was feeding slowly, his back out of water at times and his tail glittering when he swirled deliberately in the shallows to feed. The fish came almost to a stop, faced right, then moved steadily but imperceptibly forward. The bonefish seemed to be staring at the skiff.

This seemed like a tough prospect: the water was much too thin, the fish insufficiently occupied; and since he was alone, his green-and-silver shape all too clear, I couldn't imagine the bonefish would tolerate the slightest imperfection of technique.

Thomas was false-casting hard. Faced with such a good fish, his intensity was palpable throughout the boat. I told him he'd only get one shot at this fish, treading the parental thin line of reminding him of the present importance without exaggerating its difficulty. He released the cast. His loop reached out straight, turned over, and the fly fell about four inches in front of the bonefish.

The fish didn't spook. The fly sank to the bottom. Thomas moved the fly very slightly. The bonefish moved forward over it. I looked up and the bend of the rod extended all the way into the cork handle. The fish burned off through the mangrove shoots which bowed and sprang up obediently. When the fish headed out across the flat, Thomas turned to look at me over his shoulder and give me what I took to be a slightly superior grin. A short time later he boated the fish.

We were actually fishing in the middle of the Sian Ka'an biosphere reserve, over a million acres of the coast of Quintana Roo, savannas, lagoons, and seasonally flooded forest. Our simple camp met the Mexican requirement of integrating human use while preserving the complex and delicate ecosystem whose uniqueness derives not only from the phenomenon of a tropic sea inundating a vast limestone shelf, but from long human history. Every walk that Thomas and I took brought us past earthen mounds that covered Maya structures. One superb small temple has been excavated and its inspired siting caused us, hunched under its low ceilings, gazing out on the blue sea with bones and pottery at our feet, to fall silent for a good while.

Since I have been unsuccessful in bringing any formality to the job of parenting, I wondered about the matter of generations, and whether or not this concept added much to the sense of cherished companionship I had with my son. And I thought of the vast timescape implied by our immediate situation and the words of the leader of the French Huguenots when the terrible Menendez led his band of followers into a hollow in the dunes to slaughter them. "In the eyes of God," said the Huguenot, "what difference is twenty years, more or less?"

As we wandered through the barracks of an abandoned copra plantation, I saw a carved canoe paddle leaning against a wall—the kind of ancient design used to propel dugout canoes but probably the backup for an Evinrude. Inside, the walls were decorated with striking graffiti, ankle-grabbing stick ladies subjected to rear entry and the prodigious members of grinning stick hooligans, complete with rakish brimmed hats and cigarettes. There you have it.

My anxiety about Thomas's bonefishing disappeared. He did just fine. Less obsessive about fishing than I am, he had to be harassed into organizing his tackle, showing up at the skiff on time, and fishing instead of crawling around the mangroves to see what was living in there. We began to catch plenty of bonefish in a variety of situations: schooling fish in deep water, generally small, easy prey; small bunches lined up along the edge of a flat, waiting for the tide to come in and help them over; singles and small bunches, tailing and feeding, on the inside flats. Several times I looked up and saw Thomas at a distance, his rod deeply bowed and his fly line shearing an arc toward deeper water. We were happy workers on a big bonefish farm.

"Pedro, are there many permit, *unas palometas*?"

"Yes, of course,"

"Have you had many caught from your skiff?"

"No one catches many *palometas*."

"How many?"

"Maybe six this year."

Pedro stared in the direction he was poling, getting remarkable progress from the short hardwood crook with which he pushed us along. Florida guides with their graphite eighteen-footers would refuse to leave the dock with an item like this. Pedro had a faint smirk on his face, as though reading my thoughts; more likely he was feeling that the hopelessness of predictably catching a permit was his own secret. The look challenged you to try, but declined to subdue skepticism.

I feel, when searching for permit, as a bird dog must when the unsearched country ahead turns into a binary universe of sign and absence of sign. Now, I certainly couldn't expect my son to feel the same way; here in the Sian Ka'an his attention was trained on *all* the wonders around us, the sea creatures scooting out in front of the skiff in response to Pedro's skillful poling, the spectacular flying squid that sailed across our bow, the cacophonous waterfowl that addressed our passage from the secrecy of the mangroves, the superb aerobatics of frigate birds trying to rob royal terns of their catch. Graciously, Thomas offered me the first cast.

The little bay had a bottom too soft for wading. We were at a relatively low tide and the hermit crabs could be seen clinging to the exposed mangrove roots. A reddish egret made its way along the verge of thin water, head forward, legs back, then legs forward, head back until the sudden release, invisible in its speed, and the little silver fish wriggling crossways in its bill.

"Palometa," Pedro said, and we looked back to see which way his phenomenal eyes were directed. A school of permit was coming onto the sandbar that edged the flat. Once noticed, the dark shape of the school seemed busy and its underwater presence was frequently enlarged as the angular shapes of fins and tails pierced the surface. I checked to see if I was standing on my line, then tried to estimate again how much of it I had stripped out. I held the crab fly by the hook between my left thumb and forefinger and checked the loop of line. Now trailing alongside the boat, that would be my first false-cast. We were closing the distance fast and the permit were far clearer than they had been moments before. In fact, if they hadn't been so busy scouring around the bottom and

competing with one another, they could have seen us right now. The skiff ground to a halt in the sand. Pedro said that I was going to have to wade to these fish. Well, that was fine, but the few permit I have ever hooked wading had spooled me while I stood and watched them go. Furthermore, the freshwater reel I was using had lots of backing but no drag. That I'd picked it for the sporting enhancement it provided now seemed plain silly.

I climbed out, eyes locked on the fish.

"Dad!" came my son's voice. "I've got to try for these fish too!"

"Thomas, damn it, it's my shot!"

"Let me give it a try!"

"They're not going to take that bonefish fly anyway."

How could I concentrate? But now I was nearly in casting position, then heard something behind me. Thomas had bailed out of the boat and was stripping line from his reel. He was defying his father! Pedro was celebrating three thousand years of Maya family life on this bay by holding his sides and laughing. For all I knew, he had suggested my son dive into the fray.

Once in casting range, I was able to make a decent presentation and the crab landed without disturbance in front of the school. They swam right over the top of it. They ignored it. Another cast, I moved the fly one good strip. They inspected it and again refused. A third cast and a gingerly retrieve. One fish peeled off, tipped up on the fly and ate. I hooked him and he seared down the flat a short distance, then shot back into the school. Now the whole bunch was running down the flat with my fish in their midst. Thomas waded to cut them off and began to false-cast. I saw disaster staring at me as his loop turned over in front of the school and his fly dropped quietly.

"Got one!" he said amiably as his permit burned its way toward open water. Palming my whirling reel miserably, I realized why he had never been interested in a literary career. Not sick enough to issue slim volumes from the interior dark, he instead would content himself with life. He seemed to be enjoying the long runs his fish made; mine made me ill. He was still in diapers when I caught my first permit but my anxiety over a hookup had never abated.

Pedro netted my son's fish, his first permit, and waited, holding it underwater until mine was landed. Thomas came over with the net. When the fish was close, I began to issue a stream of last-minute instructions about the correct landing of a permit. He just ignored me and scooped it up.

This was unbelievable, a doubleheader on fly-caught permit. I was stunned. We had to have a picture. I asked Pedro to look in my kit for the camera. Pedro admitted that he had only had this happen once before. He groped deeper in my kit.

But I had forgotten the camera, and when Thomas saw my disappointment he grabbed my shoulders. He was grinning at me. All my children grin at me, as if I was crazy in an amusing sort of way.

"Dad," he said, "it's a classic. Don't you get it?" He watched for it to sink in. "It's better without a picture."

The permit swam away like they'd known all along that we weren't going to keep them.

Later, I stewed over his use of the word "classic." It was like the day he buried a bonefish fly in the calf of my leg. My expression then was "timeless," he had said. I would have to think about that.

"Sons," from *The Longest Silence: A Life in Fishing* by Thomas McGuane, copyright © 1999 by Thomas McGuane. Used by permission of Alfred A. Knopf, a division of Random House, Inc. UK edition published by Yellow Jersey Press. Reprinted by permission of The Random House Group Ltd.

The Iceman Fisheth

NEAL KARLEN

When my grandfather died I inherited two things from his estate: a 1940s Electrolux vacuum cleaner and a pair of Sorel ice-fishing boots. The first and only time I plugged in the vacuum, it emitted a torrent of smoke and sparks reminiscent of the rejuvenation scene in *Frankenstein,* when the mad scientist puts his bolt-necked creation through the roof of his laboratory and straight into an electrical storm.

I hit karmic gold, however, when I slipped on the ancient Arctic footwear my grandfather had worn for decades, ice fishing at four in the morning inside a tiny shack enveloped by wind-chills that could reach 60 below zero. These boots, I realized immediately, were the true essence of the man, an immigrant with the thick knuckles of a lifelong laborer who never learned English, but could read the mysteries of a Minnesota lake bottom like a master cryptologist.

He was alone in these gift-from-God skills, but not in his passion. Last year, 115,000 permits were issued for ice-fishing houses, shacks usually so tiny that they hold only enough room for a small portable heater and four anglers sitting numbly knee to knee on upturned buckets. That piece of Hollywood-ized tripe known as *Grumpy Old Men* got a few things accurately: whole towns spring up overnight when the lakes freeze to a depth of four inches, thick enough for a 200-pound person to safely walk on and dig a hole with either a manual or motorized ice auger, both of which look like corkscrews imported from Jonathan Swift's Brobdingnag.

People can drive cars onto the lakes when the ice depth reaches a foot, at which point the winter villages acquire road signs, trash pickup, speed limits, towing services, and plowed streets for easy delivery of pizza ordered via cell phone. The largest such encampment is at Mille Lacs Lake, near the Canadian border, with more than 5,000 ice houses holding an estimated 20,000 people—a population greater than that of 90 percent of Minnesota's towns. It's a weird, eerie world. At dawn, on the kind of cold Minnesota winter when your glasses seem super-glued to your head and your nostril hairs freeze, the shacks look like post-apocalyptic Hoovervilles-on-ice.

Many ice fishermen, however, prefer to travel by themselves to wherever they think the fish might be. Not even bothering with the protection of a shack, they walk or drive right onto one of the state's 15,000 lakes, dig a hole, and do battle with northern pike, bass, sunfish, and crappie. Pronounced *crop'-ee*, the crappie, despite its unfortunate nomenclature, puts up one of the best fights in fishing and tastes swell too, just watch out for the bones.

My last time ice fishing, my late grandfather's boots saved me a shred of dignity a quarter-century after he'd died. I'd done a goofy newspaper article on the lightness and general fabulosity of the latest lines of synthetic winter sportswear and had been rewarded with the expensive swag purchased by the publication, clothing I'd never buy for myself in a googol years.

So there was a part of me that thought I deserved the derision when I went to Lake Minnetonka with my father and his gaggle of grumpy old ice-fishing buddies and they started making fun of my blindingly bright, state-of-the-art, all-light-and-polyester winter wear. Respecting my elders, I made no mention of how their prototypical ice-fishing outfits made them look mummified in untold layers of drab wool dating, as the vaudeville saw goes, from when the Dead Sea was only slightly sick.

"Good boots, though," admired Abe "the Mavin" Schwartz, seventy-eight, the dean of local ice fishermen as well as the best pool and pinochle player at the local VFW. "It ain't bragging, if you can do it," Abe says about his nickname, which means "expert" in Yiddish and is emblazoned on his vanity license plates. He looked closely at my boots again, and talked to me for the first time like I wasn't an utter nitwit.

"Those are the boots of a man who knows ice fishing isn't a sport," he said, "but a punishment!"

Still, there I was, looking like an extra from *Plan 9 from Outer Space*, as the guys began their critique from the top, with my combination wool-plastic, Heidi-looking hat from some fancy designer called "Dale of Norway." Moving on down, they ridiculed my Mr. Spock live-long-and-prosper three-fingered lobster gloves, hoo-haahed when I showed them my featherweight Capilene long underwear, and were singularly unimpressed by the Gore-Tex socks sticking out of my grandfather's boots.

I'd been assured by the saleswoman that my socks were so remarkably waterproof that I could stand in a bathtub full of water and not get my feet wet. Huddled inside our ice shack, I slipped off a Sorel boot and thought she better be right as I stuck my foot in the water churning up through the hole in the ice. If she wasn't, I would never dance again. I listened for my own scream, but it never came. The socks worked.

But does it even matter? Superficially, the point of all this is to yank fish out of a ten-inch hole cut through two-foot-thick Minnesota lake ice. Existentially, it's the Nordic kin of the purification ritual of the Native American sweat lodge, except it's 60 degrees below instead of 250 above.

Personally, the best time for my father and me to get real and serious with each other is when we're alone in these pre-dawn iceboxes, staring out the window at a world that looks like a vast, foreboding moonscape. Big news and family secrets seem to pour out: I always hope my life's momentous events take place during Minnesota's five-month winter. If I'm getting divorced, or married, or engaged, or I'm moving away from Minneapolis or back to Minneapolis, I usually tell him in the ice house. He takes news of change better there.

The biggest "what if?" in the life of this usually emotionally unrevealing man came out one morning as we angled alone atop ice buckets. Once, he told me, he'd actually decided to leave Minneapolis for good.

The army had rushed him through medical school so he could be among the first waves of Americans to hit the mainland in the expected invasion of Japan toward the end of World War II. Instead, Hiroshima and Nagasaki happened and the Occupation Army assigned the twenty-one-year-old doctor to run a leper colony and a free clinic for starving Japanese on Okinawa.

During that time, he fell in love with Japan. (My mother, whom he married years later, also claims that Japanese women spoiled him forever with their kindness.) When his tour of duty was up, he and another young doctor decided to stay in Japan and open their own clinic. He sent this news home to my grandparents and a telegram, probably the only one my grandfather sent his whole life, rocketed back. All it said was:

COME HOME BUM.

So he did.

Now, several years after that revelation, he and his tough old friends in their woolens totted up how much my new ice-fishing outfit cost. With that figure, they estimated they could buy a new fish shack, a portable ice auger for drilling holes, and enough bait minnows to last through the third millennium.

sunfish

A few hours later, the painful results were in. Abe Schwartz had caught thirteen healthy-sized sunfish, my father seven. Lying on the ice was my sole catch, a puny sunny, lighter even than my Gore-Tex socks.

"Warm enough?" Abe asked me, laughing. And then he looked down at my feet.

"Nice boots, though. Those'll keep you out of trouble. Where'd you get 'em?"

From *Wishing My Father Well*

WILLIAM PLUMMER

I had been taking Nicky with me to the Gorge once or twice a year for several years. I hadn't gone yet with Sam and did not expect to in the near future. Sam was about to turn eight. I tended to take her places like the Bronx Zoo and Great Adventure. She had the aptitude, and the tools, I felt, to be a fly fisher. She had great hand-eye coordination, and a kind of patience you don't teach. I suspected that in the long run she was more suited to the pastime than her brother. But I wasn't going to rush her.

Nicky and I would go for maybe an hour or so, and leave at the first sign that he was getting bored. I would put a streamer on his line, as I did with Huey, and show him how to work it. But pretty soon I would see him standing on the rocks toying with the minnows, or over on the bank hunting frogs.

The Gorge was the most popular fly stretch in the state. It really got pounded. By midseason the fish had seen every artificial there was, and could probably tie most of them themselves. Nicky's chances of catching a trout, I figured, had to be a good deal better at Dad's club.

The club water was fished lightly after the first few weeks of the season, and the section that I had in mind for Nicky, just below the parking lot, was barely fished at any time. It was beneath the notice of most of the club members who operated almost exclusively in the upper three pools, which were loaded with trophy trout.

As we pushed through the scrim of shoulder-high grasses, dogwood and willow shoots that veiled the stretch, we spooked a great blue heron. Ordinarily, the heron discerns your presence from hundreds of yards away, but we got lucky. I watched the great gray Ichabod of a waterbird take those first few, long, running steps before launching, his neck punched out, legs dangling, as his wings slowly and massively stroked the air.

I looked over at Nick to make sure that he had seen it. He had and was smiling. He had spotted something himself. He was pointing across the stream to the opposite bank, where a mink was slipping in and out of the vegetation.

"See that?" he said.

I gave him a thumbs-up.

We stood side by side and soaked in the sunshine and the smell of the honeysuckle that laced through the streamside brush. A cedar waxwing skimmed the water. I could hear a chainsaw in the distance, but it didn't seem to disturb, so much as underscore, the quiet. As always at the club, I felt as though I had stepped out of time.

We stood there and took in the water. There was a plunge at the top of the stretch, with little scallops to be probed, if you wished, beneath the rocks. Then came a large boulder that jutted three or four feet up out of the element, creating a hoop of placid water before and aft. The boulder was a sort of marker. It stood adjacent to fifty yards of riffles that carried toward the far bank. This thin, seemingly nondescript patch of water harbored a secret, one that the heron and the mink were clearly in on. It was the nursery for the angling club water. It teemed with rainbows, brooks, and browns that seldom exceeded seven or eight inches in length and could be readily taken with a dry fly.

Caddis, as Dad would say, was the "ticket."

Caddis flies are remarkable creatures. Where mayfly larvae cling to rocks on the stream bottom or burrow in the muck, certain kinds of caddis larvae are master masons who construct little houses out of shreds of decayed leaves, grass stems, and bits of sand, which they cement together with a glue they can apparently extrude at will. Some caddis larvae even spin tiny nets among the rocks in the fast water, where they seine microscopic forms of life.

Caddis emerge in a different manner from mayflies. They don't drift to the surface, but shoot upward like a missile launched by a submarine. Some kinds of caddis can leave their cases and be airborne in little more than a second. And they must be really delicious, because trout go nuts trying to catch them. The trout come flying out of the water, sometimes three feet into the air; or they boil on the surface, trying to nab the insects as they emerge.

I tied Huey's favorite fly, the elk-hair caddis, onto Nick's line and positioned him at the top of the riffle. It was an ideal situation. You could stand in the ankle-high current and pitch down and across into the better holding water. The idea was that the fly would sink a little as it made its journey downstream; then, as the line straightened and began to pull tight, the artificial would be impelled to rise up through the water and skitter across the surface, preferably right in front of the feeding trout's nose. ("Fish wanted a skipping fly," Dad said in his diary.)

Unfortunately, these things always work better when you're diagramming them on the blackboard of your mind. For starters, Nicky, who, like me, is left-handed, kept hanging up in the foliage behind him. He was not yet capable of making a backcast over his right shoulder—something I had not taken into account. This was easily remedied. I just moved him more toward the center of the stream.

There was a bigger problem. While he took obvious pleasure in casting—he churned the air like he was making butter—Nicky did not know how to stop the rod on the cast, at both the ten and two o'clock positions. As a result, his line and fly tended to fall in a heap upon the water.

I thought of my father, how he stood patiently by my side all those years ago, as I tasked the water with a nymph. My casting must have been at least as bad as Nick's. How many times had Dad thought of stepping in and saying something? How many times had he wanted to give me a lesson right there on the stream? But he didn't. He must have made a decision to keep his mouth shut. He must have hoped I would somehow figure it out for myself.

"Nick," I said, after watching several more futile efforts, "you're rushing the cast. You've got to give the line a little time to unfurl behind you, and in front of you too."

I could feel him stiffen. But it was too late. I had chosen my course. I proceeded to show him how to do it, explaining what I was doing with as few words as possible. I could almost see him thinking, deciding whether to try it again, or to tell me that he had had enough and was ready to go home.

After a few interminable seconds, he brought his rod up toward his shoulder, lifting the line off the water, and made his backcast—right into the foliage.

"Wait!" I said. "I'll get it." I threw my own rod up onto the bank and ran over to free the fly from the bush. "Try it again."

He did, again and again. His casting completely fell apart. He stopped and wouldn't look at me.

"Nick," I said, "I've got an idea. Let's try one more thing. If it doesn't work, we leave. Okay?"

He shrugged.

"I mean it," I said. "We're out of here."

I showed him how to bring his right hand into play. How, after he made his forward cast with his left hand, to give a little tug on the line with his right. How a well-placed tug would stop the line from landing in a heap and would allow the line, leader, and fly to float naturally.

On his third or fourth cast, his fly skittered across a sub-merged rock about thirty feet below him, and there was a discernible spurt of water, made by a rising fish.

"Nick!" I shouted. "You had a strike!"

"Dad," he said. "Calm down. You scared me."

"I'm sorry, Nick," I said. "But this is exciting. You've got it beat. You're going to catch a trout."

And he did. He caught a bunch of them, little browns and rainbows and brookies. And he held the fish in his hand and stared at them, longer than he probably should have before he let them go.

"Wow, Dad, look," he said, as the first tiny brook trout settled behind his boot, to catch its breath before returning to the riffle. "He thinks I'm part of the stream."

Fishing with Dad

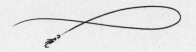

W. BRUCE CAMERON

As my father has proven to me time and time again, there is a big difference between fishing and catching fish. "Fishing" is the soul-numbing act of sitting for hours and watching a thin cobweb of nylon trail out of sight into the black depths of the lake behind the boat while nothing happens. This is best accomplished in a light rain, the boat yawing back and forth in tsunamis, your breakfast hearing voices telling it to "come on back up."

"Catching fish" is what the other boats do.

"Yo! Doin' any good?" my father bellows at passing watercraft. The fishermen hold up stringers laden with white-bellied trout.

"How 'bout you, doin' any good?" they bellow back. When you're fishing you have to talk like you never got out of third grade; I'm pretty sure it's a rule.

"Naw," my father admits. Then he points to me, like, how can I catch any fish with such a worthless son?

"Whatcha usin'?" my father hollers. I once thought this meant, "What are you taking to keep from throwing up?" like, what drugs are you using? Now I understand it to mean, "What bait have you affixed to the end of your line?"

"A Burt Reynolds!" it sounds like they yell back. I blink, wondering what in the world would possess a fish to try to swallow such a thing. Is that with the toupee, or without?

My dad smiles and nods, like, "Okay, but you're pretty damn stupid to use that kind of bait when obviously you'd be better off fishing with whatever I'm using," and waits until they are out of sight before diving into his tackle box. "Aha! I knew I had one!" he shouts, holding up what looks like my retainer from high school. "Quick, let's put this on!"

You have to wonder what the fish are thinking as our lures troll past them underwater.

FISH: "Hey, look, Ralph, isn't that Burt Reynolds's retainer swimming by at a constant speed attached to monofilament, there?"

RALPH FISH: "Hey, I think you're right! I'm gonna go bite it!"

Two hours later we are still fishing. My father keeps consulting his fish finder, which is blinking and beeping as if it has detected a fleet of Soviet submarines. "You think we're going too fast?" he asks me for the hundredth time. I shrug. I've decided the only way we're going to catch a fish is if our hooks collide with one, so if anything it seems logical to me to speed up.

"Montana, now that was an experience," my father murmurs. I carefully avoid reacting so as not to encourage another retelling of the time my father went to a catch-and-release camp in Montana. To me, catch-and-release is like paying for food at a grocery store and then putting it back. I stare at my line and will myself not to regurgitate. I am so cold I could spend a week lying in the streets of Phoenix, Arizona, and I would still be shivering. "Montana. Sure was amazing," my father chants, eyeing me carefully. I am pretty sure I'm in a coma. "Very interesting story," he remarks. "Wow, what a day. Boy. We should really talk about that one. Man. Holy smokes."

I will not talk. My brain is on catch and release. I don't even react as the tip of my father's rod bends down as sharply as a graph of the stock market, his reel making a sizzling sound in its holder. Then it occurs to me what I am seeing and I leap to my feet. "Dad! You've got a fish!"

This is such an unexpected event I feel like I've shouted something insane. Standing there, I am perfectly positioned to block my father's lunge for his rod, which means I am bodyslammed right out of the boat and into the lake, still hanging on to the fish pole in my hand.

"Hey!" I yell with an appropriate amount of surprise. I immediately begin to initiate a drowning sequence.

My father, of course, is busy pulling in his catch, and seems remarkably uninterested in the fact that his son is fast falling both behind and below his boat.

"Hey!" I announce again.

"Hold on to the rod!" he shouts encouragingly.

My clothes are filling with water and it is becoming increasingly difficult to picture myself breathing. He wants me to cling to something that feels like it is tied to the bottom of the lake. Screw the rod, it's life I'm concentrating on holding on to. "Help!" I shriek, since "Hey!" seemed to convey the wrong message. I get ready to have my whole life pass before my eyes, but all that comes to me is that I forgot to carry the trash out to the curb this morning.

Then something smacks me behind the ear. I look up, blinking, and see that my father has steered over to me and is wielding the fishnet. "Why are you hitting me in the head?" I demand peevishly.

"Grab it!" he commands earnestly. I flail out, catch the net, and am pulled over to the side of the boat. With a lot of strenuous gasping, we manage to get me aboard.

I fall to the floor and leak water, panting. "The fish?" I finally manage to choke.

He shakes his head.

"The rod?" he asks.

I make the same negative gesture. Our defeat is so profound that we don't even speak while he turns the boat toward shore. We're done for the day. We pass other fishermen and don't even ask if they're doin' any good.

Half an hour later we're approaching the docks. I've brought up all the water I swallowed and returned it to the lake, and the sun is actually getting ready to make a comeback. "Looks like we're going to have to wait a bit," my dad remarks, pointing to the long line of watercraft awaiting their turn at the boat ramp. He cuts the engine and we drift a bit, not saying anything.

"So," I say finally. "Tell me about that fishing trip you took to Montana."

Ice Fishing

TERESA CADER

Today my father crouches above the ice on Black Hill Lake
and the bass, spinning in slivers of winter sunlight,
swim to the surface with the aura of dreams,
in their speckled eyes the slow, ominous stare of memory.
Next to the crosshatched hole in the ice, the bucket
fills with fish, the water turns filmy with blood

and the fluttering gills of the bass, jagged and bloody,
heave against each other. In the white cove of the lake,
the wind is shuddering now, my father lifts the bucket
into the air and fifteen bass glide into light,
then sink, startled, into the water. He has memorized
this give-and-take, the way I imagine he dreams

he is a young boy again, and the one relentless dream
of his old age begins its slow ascent in his blood.
The voices are dim, inarticulate, but he remembers
standing in his father's rowboat on a mountain lake
in 1914, the flash of German gunfire lighting
his face, and the first drops of rain hitting the bucket

in the bow of the boat, and bending to hide the bucket
beneath his coat so no one could hear. In the dream,
he is nearing shore when a white-haired man lightly
taps his shoulder, and when he turns, blood
from the old man's gunshot wounds seeps into the lake,
colors the water, the sky, his face, red, even his memory,

so that he no longer recognizes, or even remembers
the face of his grandfather above the stern. The bucket
fills and refills and the fissured ice on the lake
grows thin and soft. In the midst of his daydreaming
he doesn't notice the way his footprints fill with fish blood
and in the clear air in late morning, the March light

is strong enough to melt the ice. In a crackle of light,
he hears the hole split wider, the water surge, and remembers
his fishing rod poised on the edge of the ice, blood
spilling into the water, and throws a half-full bucket
into the air, the way he'd thrown his childhood dreams
into the arms of his dead grandfather on the lake

and everything, water, harsh light, the metal bucket,
converges as it did in 1914, memories and dreams
swirling like blood beneath the ice on Black Hill Lake.

A Border Boyhood

From *Angling Sketches*

ANDREW LANG

A fisher, says our father Izaak, is like a poet: he "must be born so." The majority of dwellers on the Border are born to be fishers, thanks to the endless number of rivers and burns in the region between the Tweed and the Coquet—a realm where almost all trout-fishing is open, and where, since population and love of the sport have increased, there is now but little water that merits the trouble of putting up a rod.

Like the rest of us in that country, I was born an angler, though under an evil star, for, indeed, my labors have not been blessed, and are devoted to fishing rather than to the catching of fish. Remembrance can scarcely recover, "nor time bring back to time," the days when I was not busy at the waterside; yet the feat is not quite beyond the power of Mnemosyne. My first recollection of the sport must date from about the age of four. I recall, in a dim brightness, driving along a road that ran between banks of bracken and mica-veined rocks, and the sunlight on a shining bend of a highland stream, and my father, standing in the shallow water, showing me a huge yellow fish, that gave its last fling or two on the grassy bank. The fish seemed as terrible and dangerous to me as to Tobit, in the Apocrypha, did that ferocious half-pounder which he carries on a string in the early Italian pictures. How oddly Botticelli and his brethren misconceived the man-devouring fish, which must have been a crocodile strayed from the Nile into the waters of the Euphrates! A half-pounder! To have been terrified by a trout seems a bad beginning; and, thereafter, the mist gathers over the past, only to lift again when I see myself, with a crowd of other little children, sent to fish, with crooked pins, for minnows, or "baggies" as we called them, in the Ettrick.

If our parents hoped that we would bring home minnows for bait, they were disappointed. The party was under the command of a nursery governess, and probably she was no descendant of the mother of us all, Dame Juliana Berners. We did not catch any minnows, and I remember sitting to watch a bigger boy, who was angling in a shoal of them when a parr came into the shoal, and we had bright visions of alluring that monarch of the deep. But the parr disdained our baits, and for months I dreamed of what it would have been to capture him, and often thought of him in church. In a moment of profane confidence my younger brother once asked me:

"What do *you* do in sermon time? I," said he in a whisper—"mind you don't tell—I tell stories to myself about catching trout." To which I added similar confession, for even so I drove the sermon by, and I have not "told"—till now.

The complete text of this piece was obtained from Project Gutenberg: www.gutenberg.org/etext/2022.

From *Misadventures of a Fly Fisherman*

JACK HEMINGWAY

In the years following my parents' divorce until my mother and Paul Mowrer were married, when we moved back to the States permanently, I had practically become a trans-Atlantic commuter. I spent the greater part of every summer with Papa and Pauline, and though they kept an apartment in Paris and used it periodically, their principal residence was in Key West, at the very tip of the Florida Keys.

Sometimes I traveled alone under the supervision of ship's personnel, but usually I went with a friend or relative who would deliver me into Papa's safekeeping at the docks in New York.

The first of these expeditions to New York stands out especially because the memory was heightened by an unusual incident. After leaving the docks and the cab ride to Scribner's on Fifth Avenue, there was a pleasant visit with Max Perkins followed by a restaurant lunch where I listened with fascination to Papa and Perkins's men's talk. Next to Papa's burly figure, Mr. Perkins seemed a reed of a man, with a schoolmasterish bearing and a total lack of egotism. I remember his calm, low voice—quite a contrast to Papa's—as they talked of books and writers, though what they said was beyond my understanding.

Afterward, I took a bus ride on the open top of a double-decker Fifth Avenue bus to within a couple blocks of the Perkins' brownstone where I was left for the rest of a very pleasant afternoon with Mrs. Perkins and had the run of the garden while the sun still shone, then took my customary nap.

That evening Perkins accompanied us down to the train at Penn Station where we boarded the Pullman bound for Miami and the Florida Keys. At Trenton, a bit before Philadelphia, the conductor delivered a telegram to Papa. Papa explained to me that Grandfather Hemingway was dead and that he must go to the funeral and take care of things for the family. I had nothing to worry about since I would be left in the care of the Pullman porter who would see that I got my meals and went to bed on time, and would see me safely to Key West where Pauline would be waiting. I was, as yet, unacquainted with death, and these events didn't seem to me, an experienced world traveler of five, at all unusual. Papa did not tell me then that Grandfather had shot himself in the head with his old Civil War pistol.

After a few months in Key West, we all returned to France

via Havana and Spain; but when summer came, off I went again to Key West: this time for what was to be the first of many car trips west with Papa. After traveling via Piggott, Arkansas, to visit Pauline's family, the Pfeiffers, where I was taken in with great kindness, love, and affection, we took the Model A Ford Coupe, with its running boards and rumble seat, west through the center of the country into the Rocky Mountains and on to the L-T Ranch near Cooke City, Montana. These trips west were always great adventures. From grandfather Paul Pfeiffer I learned that being a step-grandson of the bank president and owner of the cotton gin, as well as the largest landowner thereabouts, was a privileged position which entitled one to the luxury of "charging" sodas and sundaes, and any number of wondrous goodies that had not existed in France, at the local drugstore. And there were other spectacles and adventures on every hand as we headed west.

It was the Depression and hard times were upon the land most of those years until the outbreak of World War II. Papa was becoming a successful writer during a period when a great majority of people felt a deep financial crunch. The parts of the Deep South through which we drove seemed to be populated only by undernourished-looking black families in run-down shanties, and I don't remember ever seeing much change in that regard until well after the war.

Papa was naturally generous and friendly, especially when he was away from the intellectual coterie of his writing life. Whenever there was room, we would squeeze in some riders along the way who couldn't afford the price of a train ticket. They weren't called hitchhikers yet. Papa would always talk freely with them and get their story out of them. There were hard-luck stories of every ilk and most with the ring of truth. For me it was learning that couldn't be duplicated elsewhere. There seemed always to be some humor and hope though, no matter how depressing the tale.

One year we had a nearly very serious accident. We had left the Gulf Coast after a night's stay in New Orleans where we'd paid our usual visit to the oyster bar and the shooting gallery near the Monteleone Hotel where we always stayed. We were on the way to Baton Rouge when a smallish hog suddenly started across the road in front of the car. Papa always drove fast in those days and it was a close call but he managed to hit the hog with only a glancing blow and caused only the most superficial damage to the car while inflicting sudden death on the hapless hog. Now, that hog was no fat, prime specimen of its kind. It was in about as poor shape as a hog can be and still qualify for the title of hog.

Its owner rushed out of the roadside woods yelling, "That's my prize hog you just done kilt, mister, and he's going to cost you twenty bucks!"

Papa parried back, "You deliberately pushed that hog out onto the road when you saw the car coming, and it's the most worthless-looking hog I ever saw."

Papa and the man settled for five dollars and then Papa instructed me to be on the lookout from then on, whenever there was cover along the road, for what we called "hog launchers." We decided it was an honorable profession during hard times and that you just had to be wary of them when traveling through prime hog-launching country.

It became a tradition on these journeys that, in order to avoid getting in the habit of using bad language and cussing and telling dirty jokes, there was an established time in the latter part of every evening when, for an hour, we were permitted full license in all these respects. When my younger brother, Patrick, was old enough to come along this became especially important because we would tend to get pretty wild. The situation was even more extreme when Patrick and I rode in the rumble seat and Papa and Pauline were up front. It may not have been pure coincidence that this period of condoned verbal misbehavior took place when it was time for Papa's first drink of the day, which I was trained early on to mix for him with just the right measure of two big fingers of scotch and little enough water not to drown it. Ice was used when available.

Among the more ludicrous, but never to be forgotten, creations of these sessions was "The Famous Bathroom." This was scatology carried to its ultimate extreme. "TFB" was a museum which we would create for the preservation of fecal specimens not only of all the various species of living creatures, but of famous historical characters as well. Our imaginations knew no bounds in this project, and during the time when such talk was forbidden, we often spent time planning for the dirty hour. It was not an unhealthy activity and it actually opened the doors to questions it is sometimes difficult to approach one's own parents about, although Papa never condoned or liked conventional dirty jokes.

The first real Western mountains we crossed on that first drive were the Bighorns in Wyoming. The road then was just a thin dirt ribbon and much of it passed between sheer cliff on one side and pure precipice on the other. On one stretch we met a rarity in those days, another car coming up the grade toward us. It took some serious maneuvering on the edge of the precipice while the other car squeezed between us and the cliff. I remember being nearly paralyzed with fear sitting next to the window on the outside. The next day, going through Yellowstone from the south entrance, we were held up for hours by repair work on the winter-ravaged road. The worst, however, was the fourteen miles of mostly corduroy road from just outside Cooke City to the ranch. We lost our oil pan and finally had to be pulled out by a team of horses. In later years, after the construction of the Cooke City/Red Lodge Highway, getting to the ranch was a snap, although the new highway excavation near Cooke City triggered land and mud slides which adversely affected the clarity and fishing quality of the Clark's Fork River for many years thereafter.

Lawrence Nordquist's L-T Ranch was situated on the south side of the valley of the Clark's Fork. Now it is reached by crossing a wooden bridge after coming off the Cooke City/Red Lodge Highway and then crossing a series of broad meadow pastures and fields of oats to the ranch house, with its cluster of log cabins scattered through the grove of lodgepole pine.

That first year we arrived via the "old" road which crossed the stream by a ford in its shallow headwaters close to Cooke City and skirted myriad swamps, rock falls, and finally ended crossing the sagebrush flat beyond One Mile Creek near the ranch. The main building was typical Western guest ranch— very simple but clean and piney, with a big living room with lots of chairs, and books left by former guests. The lodge had a couch or two and a big dining room where overabundant but delicious meals were served. I was alone, that trip, with Papa and Pauline and had a little room of my own in their cabin. The Franklin stove was in their room, and my first job in the morning was to put some of the kerosene-soaked sawdust and a few small logs on the fire to get the cabin warmed up.

After breakfast at the main lodge, Papa and Pauline would get their fishing tackle ready and, after getting the horses saddled, they would take off with a pack lunch to some point on the river, usually several miles downstream. I was left pretty much to my own devices and the ranch was well organized for kids.

There must have been three or four other children there, though I think I was the youngest. Ivan Skinner, the top wrangler, saw to it that we all had proper-fitting saddles, and within a few days we had all learned to saddle up by ourselves and knew our horses pretty well. I was blessed with a white horse speckled in fine-grained liver. He was called Pinky. He was hard to saddle because he would bloat up his stomach when I tried to cinch him up tight. Consequently, I had numerous accidents when I would end up beneath him; but I eventually learned to give him a slap or a good knock just before the cinching so he'd let out the air long enough to get the job done right.

Learning to ride was fun and, at first, consisted mainly of long rides in line following one of the wranglers to some nearby lake or stream, or up the squaw trail to get over the rimrock and up into the Hurricane Mesa country where Billy Sidley's grandfather had his monument plaque and where they had scattered his ashes. I thought it was a beautiful place to have your ashes scattered and thought about having the same thing done for myself someday.

Billy was my best friend at the ranch and helped initiate me to the tricks of being a proper horse wrangler, as we like to think of ourselves. He was only a couple of years older than I, but he'd been coming out to the ranch from Chicago for several summers already and knew all the ropes. His family had been coming for years, and the ash-scattered grandfather had built a fine log cabin for their family down across the meadow on a small sagebrush promontory overlooking a beautiful riffle of the Clark's Fork. In later years the Sidleys stopped coming out and Papa was able to rent their cabin, which was much better suited to his writing since it was situated well away from the many distractions and noises of the main corral and ranch buildings.

Another job I had that year was to gather wild strawberries

which grew in abundance, rare for the species, in the woods around our cabin. In the cabins, we had those old-fashioned heavy glass tumblers, and I had to fill two of these as first priority. Pauline would then crush the strawberries into the bottom of the tumbler and add gin for their first-of-the-day "ranch cocktails." I took my strawberries straight. They were so sweet they needed not the least sprinkle of sugar.

One day Pinky done me wrong. We kids had been playing horseback tag in the irrigated pasture down by the river. The horses were tired and when we came into the corral everyone but me unsaddled and brushed off their mounts. I made the unfortunate mistake of deciding to ride Pinky to the cabin to fetch something or other and he decided to revolt. At first he refused to move, and then when I gave him a good whack of the leather quirt, he took off like a scalded cat right through the compound of cabins. That would have been all right, since he'd have just run himself out in a little time, but he headed for the place where Mrs. Nordquist hung out the laundry on wires strung between the pines. I managed to duck the first wire, but the second caught me right across the chest and took me right out of the saddle. The scar is gone now, but I can understand why everyone was so concerned. That wire could just as easily have taken my head off, and that would have been the end of this tale.

On the days that Papa worked, Pauline would sometimes go on the trail rides. This was my cue to stay home. Not because I didn't want to be with Pauline, but because I knew that Papa would go fishing near the ranch by himself when he was through work. I knew he really wanted to be alone, but, on the other hand, I really wanted to learn about trout fishing. He knew I was just hanging around waiting to be asked to join him so he could teach me how to cast and all the other great mysteries. He didn't, so I tried sneaking up to the river where he would be wading in his chest-waders in the fast, clear, green-tinged water.

He spotted me right off and came over to the bank.

"You know, Schatz, trout spook awfully easily—"

"I'm sorry, Papa, I only wanted—"

"If you really want to watch just stay back a little from the bank. You mustn't move around until I go further down. Then move very slowly and stay low."

"Yes, Papa!"

"That way the trout won't spook."

I tried to become a part of the shadows along the stream side.

I had to settle for this role for the rest of our stay that year, except for the last few days when I was rewarded with an opportunity to fish with Pauline's already set-up outfit with a single hook which was an old, worn fly that Papa trimmed the dressing off of so I could impale a grasshopper and fish it in the swirling back eddies that Papa pretty much ignored while he was fishing his two- or three-fly wet-fly rig through the riffles.

My purported patience during the endless periods of being a watcher had been a sham. I had darn near died of impatience to have a real go at it myself, and the trout that Papa caught were so beautiful compared to my Grand Morin minnows that my desire to capture one became an obsession.

Nevertheless, I learned a lot about casting and about playing fish once they were hooked. Papa was a pretty straightforward wet-fly fisherman. He used Hardy tackle and his leaders were already made up with three flies. His favorites were a McGinty for the top, a *cock-y-bondhu* for the middle, and a woodcock green and yellow for the tail fly. He sometimes fished with single-eyed flies and added a dropper. At the ranch, for these, he preferred Hardy's worm fly and the shrimp fly.

Ninety percent of the time, Papa was an across and down-stream caster whose team of flies swam or skittered across the current so that a taking fish pretty much hooked himself. He played the fish gently and well and with the necessary calm that eliminates hurrying a fish too fast or playing it too long, which is just as great a sin.

He seldom failed to land his trout except for the rare double-header when one or both fish were often lost. He taught me how to clean them and insisted that the part along the back-bone which looks like coagulated blood, which ought to be the aorta but is in reality the trout's kidney, be left if the fish weren't to be kept too long before eating. He said this improved the flavor.

He used a woven grass basket rather like a shopping bag from Hardy's for a creel and laid the trout in it on fresh leaves of grass or branches of fern. The creel was dampened in the river and the evaporation kept the fish cool. "Never waste fish, Schatz, it's criminal to kill anything you aren't going to eat," Papa told me. Then he impressed on me how important it was never to waste fish or game by not taking proper care of it.

The trout Papa caught were seldom cooked in the ranch house kitchen. He preferred to cook them himself, usually for breakfast, on top of the stove in the cabin in a frying pan with lots of butter and lemon and salt and pepper. He always added the lemon while the fish were frying, claiming this gave them a better taste.

My immediate problem, now that I was rod in hand with a six-foot leader and the hopper impaled on the fly hook, was that the grasshopper wouldn't sink, because of its natural buoyancy. I had no idea then about floating flies, nor did I know about lead-split shot used for sinking a bait or a fly. With just the leader and hardly any line extending beyond the rod tip, I flipped the hopper out toward the center of the whirlpool, and then it was pulled under into the vortex and I immediately saw my line twitch, and I gave a powerful yank and, unlike the minnows which had flown out of the water in the same circumstances, I found myself with a bent rod tip and a very active, strong, living creature doing its best to get to the middle of the stream.

I tried to emulate what I had watched Papa do, and with luck on my side, I finally landed the most beautiful fish I had ever seen. It was a rainbow cutthroat hybrid about eleven inches long and looked enormous to me as I pounced on it on the sandy backwater shore.

It's hard to imagine what a miracle that first trout seemed to me. Everything about it was perfect, and after the long weeks of watching in frustration as my father fished, it truly seemed the ultimate reward. That trout was consumed in its entirety by me at the ranch house that night, amidst much ado. It was the first of many from that lovely river, although the next few days were filled with various frustrations, some of which were overcome.

I just continued to fish places exactly like the one where I had had my initial success. Experiments in different types of water were unsuccessful, but the seed had been well planted and it had grown into an overwhelming desire to fish for trout—a desire which remains just as strong to this day.

It sometimes wonder if I'd have retained my enthusiasm to such a degree, or at all, if my father had followed the usual path of providing me with all the necessaries and plying me with detailed instructions and supervision. I know he wanted me to love fishing and hunting, and I believe that he deliberately set about to make me really want to do it on my own initiative. Tennis parents and stage mothers should take note. The kid has got to want to do it, not just to please the parent, but for himself.

That's Life

PETER KAMINSKY

Lily and I, with nothing much to do, took a stroll down the beach, about a mile, to Georgica Pond. A southwest breeze tempered the withering heat and humidity and the surge of the incoming tide sloshing around our ankles felt splendidly cool. We talked of her friends at summer camp (sorely missed), her sister's departure for college (ditto) mixed in with the "unimportant" small talk that makes idle summer hours so delicious.

Just as we were about to return to the beach house of our friend, Josh Feigenbaum, some movement caught my attention. About two hundred yards west of us, a swarm of terns began to mass and flutter their wings as they held position over something going on beneath them. Then one dove, and another, and another. They wheeled and reformed for another sortie, and another, and another.

It could only mean one thing: "Bluefish for sure, Lily, let's grab a rod!"

Fumbling through Josh's tackle box I retrieved a productive lure, the Hopkins, with a rusty, but still sharp, treble hook. I tied on a wire leader, clipped on the lure and we sprinted down the beach. When we reached the mayhem at the water's edge, you could see baitfish leap from the water in a spray of silver droplets and, like deathly shadows behind them, hundreds of bluefish, feeding with ravenous abandon.

Lily, who casts reasonably, could not quite reach the action, so I took the rod from her, tossed a cast into the eye of the storm, and handed her the rod. As instructed, she reeled in. Within moments a bluefish struck hard.

Next came the "What do I do now?" moment that all novice anglers experience when the pleasant enough idea of fishing becomes the reality of a living thing fighting for its life at the other end of the line.

Often, people will point the rod at the fish and reel in nonstop. This puts none of the force of the rod into the fight, and gives the fish the opportunity to pull more and more line from the reel while you strip its gears. This is a natural, and by far the most common, reaction.

To her credit, even in the heat of battle Lily followed my instructions to pull up and reel down, thus tiring the fish and recovering line.

Then came the next "What do I do?" moment as the fish emerged from the sea foam and flopped around on the beach.

Lily opted for returning the fish, so, with some difficulty I extracted the lure from its mouth and released it.

The birds followed the school slowly eastward. We changed the lure for a single hook.

Now the action was directly in front of a group of middle-aged ladies strolling along the beach.

We cast again and Lily fought another fish to the beach. This time, though, I wanted to keep it for dinner.

"Get me a nice piece of driftwood," I asked and Lily ran above the high-tide mark, then returned with a cudgel-sized stick. I whacked the fish over the head, killing it instantly. Lily's mood changed at this point. She was disturbed by the violence and felt some sympathy for the fish.

"What kind of fish are they?" one of the ladies asked.

"Blues. Would you like to catch one?"

"I never have, but why not?"

I cast again, handed over the rod, and the woman, who introduced herself as Patricia, caught her first bluefish. I clunked this one too and Lil and I returned home.

"I like the catching part but I don't like the killing," Lily said. My protestations that we were about to have a great meal of the freshest fish did nothing to counteract her misgivings.

At home I filleted the fish and, to justify myself by making a point about the circle of life, or something like that, I took the carcasses down to the water and tossed them in, explaining to Lily that this would feed other fish and birds.

She was unmoved.

Then, as I washed out the sink, my wife noticed some of the little silversides that our bluefish had gulped down for their last supper. "Look, Lily," I said as I showed her a palmful of dead baitfish, "the bluefish must have killed a thousand of these little fish. I mean, it's as much a killer as we are."

She took the small fish, examined them, and returned them to me.

I returned to the kitchen, heated some butter in a pan, seasoned the fish with salt and pepper, and cooked it in just a few minutes. Then it was a matter of spreading some mayo on toast, laying some lettuce on top followed by a slice of tomato, plump with August sweetness, and finally the cooked fish. The result was a few fine-looking Bluefish, Lettuce, and Tomato sandwiches. After some visible internal debate, Lily picked up a half sandwich, took a bite and pronounced our Long Island B-L-T a success.

A New-Moon Bass

From *A Place on the Water*

JERRY DENNIS

On summer nights the largemouth bass that had been driven into hiding all day were on patrol, and hungry. If you stood on the shore in the darkness and listened beyond the racket of belching frogs and chirping tree insects, you could sometimes hear the sudden explosive sounds of bass feeding on the surface. Small creatures were dying out there.

My father was by nature a solitary angler. He had little tolerance for companions who talked when they should have been fishing, who clattered gear in the bottom of the boat, who made sloppy, ill-planned casts. In a land of trout streams and lakes filled with northern pike and walleyes, he was an anomaly, a bass fisherman. More: He was a night fisherman.

In those days our portion of the country was not often recognized as bass territory. Walleye fishermen on slow days sometimes trolled crankbaits along the gravel bars and caught smallmouths, but largemouth bass almost never attracted attention. They were considered an underclass, ranked below smallmouths, which were ranked below walleyes, which in turn were ranked below the brown trout and brook trout of the dry-fly streams. Largemouths were crude. Southerners called them "hogs" and "bucketmouths" and regarded them with reverence, but in northern Michigan, in the warm water of summer, many anglers believed they grew stunted and feeble-minded. They were treated little better than bloated, slightly glorified panfish.

largemouth bass

But Dad knew better. He had begun fishing the hidden lakes in the quiet corners of Grand Traverse, Benzie, and Lee-lanau counties when he came home from the Army with a serious need to spend some time on the water, years before I was born. He worked his way through two or three dozen lakes and ponds, learning them the way a scholar learns obsolete languages, and when he found the lake that suited him best he made up his mind to someday own a piece of its shoreline.

He was a restless young man. During that first six months after he left the Army he held seven jobs, and was on his way to California in search of better prospects when the car he and a friend were driving broke down while they were in Grand Rapids, still in Michigan. It took all their money to get it running again. With their last tank of gas they drove to Flint, got jobs at an auto plant, and moved temporarily into a friend's apartment. After a day and a half of factory work my father quit and went to work for a company that installed radio antennas, but the company soon went bankrupt. Between jobs he met the woman who would be my mother.

In 1959 my father moved his reluctant wife and his five- and three-year-old sons from a new house in a pleasant neighborhood in Flint to a drafty, cold, spider-infested cottage on a lake in northern Michigan. He had become a police officer on the Flint City Police Department by then, but after five years he had seen far too many murder-suicides and fatal automobile accidents, and was more anxious than ever to move north and buy his place on the water. A few months after moving to the cottage my brother and I would always remember as "The Spider House," we moved to another house on the same lake; a few years later we moved again, to a larger house on a larger lake.

Dad never looked back. He went to work repairing appliances for Montgomery Ward, then selling copy machines and overhead projectors, and devoted summer evenings to the pursuit of largemouth bass.

The summer after I turned eight years old I was struck with a passion for fishing so powerful it left room for almost nothing else in my life. I remember the moment it happened. I was sitting straddling a forked branch in a maple in the yard of our house on Silver Lake, peeling an orange. The day was bright and warm, the breeze delicious. I peeled off pieces of the orange skin and dropped them one at a time, watching them fall to the ground. Some of the pieces fell straight down, others struck branches and bounced, spinning and tumbling away. I looked through the shifting, shadowy leaves of the tree toward the lake—it was blue and ruffled, and there were boats sitting motionless on it—and suddenly I longed to hold a fishing rod attached to a fish. For just a moment I felt the bucking and lunging of the fish as surely as if I was fighting a six-pound pike. I had fished many times before that, alone and with my father, but I had never been so aware of the sensations involved. The urge to duplicate that feeling was irresistible. I finished eating the orange, climbed down from the tree, and went to the lake to cast lures off our dock. I fished every day after that, all summer. Because I was too young to operate the outboard motor myself, I spent the days casting from the dock or from shore, waiting for my father to come home from work. At night I hounded him mercilessly.

He tolerated my enthusiasm the way a mature dog tolerates a new pup in the household. And I was a very energetic pup, overflowing with the joy of new life, willing to throw all thought and prudence aside for the pleasure of an exquisite hour of fishing with him. If I was not allowed to join him—very late at night, or if he was out with my uncles and there was no room in the boat—I pouted and grew petulant. But the injustice was always forgiven the next time he looked up at me and said, "Want to do some casting?"

In some ways the critics were right. Those Yankee bass did not grow especially large. Most were two or three pounds, and the six-pounders my father landed once or twice each summer were truly bragging size, or would have been if he had been the sort to brag.

But to me it made no difference that our fish could not compare to the belly-slung hogs of Texas and Florida. It was enough just to be fishing, to be immersed in darkness, surrounded by the rich, textured odors of bottomland mixed with decomposing vegetation and the acrid scent of insect repellent, listening to the chirruping sounds of night creatures surrounding the shore like a crazed, atonal symphony.

New moon was the best time. Total darkness, my father said, would make the bass secure and careless, urge them away from cover, make them more eager to investigate disturbances on the surface. In the ink-black darkness of a new-moon night a big bass would forget hard-won lessons and would be as reckless and enthusiastic as a twelve-incher. He would attack anything clumsy enough to fall on the surface of the lake, his domain.

My father's tackle box was ancient, large, and made of steel, with foldout trays divided into compartments that had been lined with sheets of cork. He owned dozens of bass plugs—red-and-white Bass-Orenos, glass-eyed Pikies, Hula Poppers—but as far as he was concerned there was only one lure for catching bass at night: the Arbogast Jitterbug. He had Jitterbugs in every size and color, but he always preferred large ones with a frog finish. Once rigged with Jitterbugs, we were set. We could pass an entire night in contentment, casting into the darkness and listening to the gurgling music of the retrieve.

I realized that night fishing was primarily an adult activity, and that it involved a world too big and potentially dangerous for children. I only fished at night because my father was there. Without him I spent my time in shallow water on bright afternoons, water you could see through to the bottom, near the rowboat pulled up on shore with its oars trailing in the sand. During the day, I caught bluegills and rock bass and adolescent largemouths possessing the same degree of inexperience and eagerness as I. In the daytime I never believed I would catch a large bass. But night fishing was different. At night bass could be as large and abundant as your imagination allowed. They swam in a world so dark and mysterious, so ripe with potential, that I knew they could be caught.

One night we fished a broad, shallow bay far down the shore from our house, a place I had seldom visited at night. I knew from daytime excursions that lily pads clogged the inner shoreline, and that along one edge ancient logs and stumps formed a border above a drop-off to deep water. We moved by oar, my father in control, and progressed slowly, one stroke at a time, until we had cast our way around the perimeter of the bay, from the stumps to the lily pads to the relatively open water on the far side. It was there, near the open water, that I was introduced into the adult world of night fishing.

An extrasensory awareness sometimes emerges when you're fishing at night. I've noticed it in recent years casting streamers on rivers for trout, trolling the flats by moonlight for walleyes, probing the undercut banks of a small stream for the brown trout that live there, but it has never been so apparent or powerful as that summer night on the lake with my father. I was not a good caster. I was inexperienced and clumsy and too eager, and yet, somehow, in the darkness I could exceed my limitations. My casts were long and faultless, always landing (I imagined) at the edges of the lily pads or in the pockets between the stumps. It was too dark to see my own hand before my face yet I knew when I had made a good cast. I retrieved the lure in fits and starts, with intervals of rest that lasted as long as I could bear to wait. Looking hard into the darkness I imagined the lure so vividly—surging, gurgling across the water, leaving a V-wake of ripples pointing to it like directional arrows—that I knew when the large bass became aware of it, when it turned in the water to focus on the odd, splashing creature on the surface, when it drifted up from the bottom and away from the weeds where it had been hovering, waiting. The realization was electric, frightening. My father felt it also. He stopped reeling, perhaps stopped breathing.

Even the shore creatures seemed to sense the intention of the bass and quieted in anticipation.

I gave the Jitterbug one more twitch, a mere tightening of the line that sent the tiniest ripple of life into the water, and suddenly I wanted to yank the lure out of the water. I wanted to be safely on shore, in our house, in a room bright with lamps and a blue television screen. I did not want the drama of the night or the terrible expectancy of knowing that something large and violent was about to attack. I was afraid of the moment when the silence would be shattered by the strike and my father would shout "Whoa!" or "There!" while I shouted something far less articulate and reared back on my rod in reflex and fear.

Then, at that very moment, while I feared that it would happen, the water blew up.

I struck, reeled madly to be sure there was no slack, then struck again to set the hook, as I had been taught. By the sound and the volume of water displaced and now the heavy weight against the rod, I was sure it was not an ordinary bass. My father reeled his lure and line from the water.

"Keep the rod high," he said.

It ran, surging deep, and I knew I did not want to fight this fish. It was simply too big. I reeled futilely, the drag slipping while line was pulled out by the fish. Then I could feel the line rising and knew the bass was coming to the surface.

"Dad!"

It thrashed the water, too big to jump free, and wallowed

half-submerged, shaking its head, throwing spray that sounded like bucket-water flung in the darkness. The bass dove and I knew I would lose it. It would wrap around thickets of weeds and break the line.

"Dad! Take the rod! It's going for the weeds!"

"You're doing fine. Keep the rod high."

"I don't want to lose it! You bring it in!"

"You hooked it, you can land it or lose it yourself."

"Dad!"

"Just let him fight, let him wear himself out."

It's strange that I don't recall other bass caught those nights. I know there were many, because my father still talks about them, but for me the nights have all blended into that one night, and all the other fish have been forgotten. There is a photograph enlarged and framed in my parents' house of my brother and me hoisting the five-pound largemouth between us, my brother there because we woke him when we returned with the fish and he wanted to share the glory. I remember the sudden flash of the camera, and the spot of brilliance that blinded me for minutes afterward, and my mother laughing and saying it was the biggest bass she had ever seen, though I knew even then that it wasn't. I remember too the relief that had flooded over me when the large, black creature in the water was finally swept into my father's landing net and swung into the boat where it thumped against the aluminum two, three times, then was still. And I remember my father switching on the flashlight and shining it on the fish, seeing it illuminated suddenly, sheening with water, its mouth clamped down, even in defeat, on the little frog-colored lure.

By most standards it was not a trophy bass, but when you considered those five pounds in relation to my seventy-five pounds the fish gained significance. My father would have needed to catch one weighing nearly fifteen pounds to equal the achievement.

"It's fat as a piglet," he said when he had it in the net, but to me it looked bigger yet, fat as a sow. I could not imagine a larger bass living in our lake. To this day I have not caught one that can match it.

From *A Place on the Water* by Jerry Dennis. Copyright © 1993 by the author and reprinted with permission of St. Martin's Press, LLC.

Doing It Right

ED ZIERALSKI

Lori Signs has been around the world eleven times, worked as a road manager for the likes of Paul McCartney, Madonna, George Michael and ZZ Top.

A woman does all that by the time she's forty, and it's a good bet that it takes a bunch to impress her.

But then, this is the same Lori Signs who learned to fish and hunt from her father and is passing on the great traditions of fishing and hunting to her fourteen-year-old niece, Heather Keznetzoff.

Leaha and Javad Trew, Paul Duclos, all you world-record bass chasers out there, listen up. Keznetzoff and Signs followed all the International Game Fish Association's rules to the letter, and now Heather has a junior world record for bluegill, a 2-pound, 2-ouncer caught last year at Lake Barrett.

Keznetzoff and Signs were fishing from a rental boat at Barrett last April 27 when Keznetzoff hooked what she thought was one of Barrett's famous largemouth bass. A huge bluegill will do that, and this one was gigantic. It attacked a yellow Mister Twister with all the vengeance of a big bass.

bluegill

"I thought it was a bass by the way it was fighting," Keznetzoff said.

Added Signs: "I thought it was a bass, too, because of the way it fought, and when we saw it, it was so black-looking."

Soon, Keznetzoff had the fish aboard, and that's when her aunt went to work.

"I've been going for a world-record fish for ten years, so what happens, my niece gets lucky and pulls one in," Signs said, laughing. "It was really hard to let it go, but all fish have to be released at Barrett, so we weighed it, got some witnesses, took lots of pictures and released it."

Signs has two BogaGrip scales that have been certified by the IGFA. She weighed it in front of a couple of fishermen who motored over to witness it. She got their names and phone numbers. She took countless pictures of it with a tape measure alongside it and around its girth. It was 11 inches long, but sported an amazing potbelly that stretched the tape 13 inches.

Had Leaha Trew done all those things with her supposed 22-pound, 8-ounce largemouth last year at Spring Lake in Santa Rosa, or had Duclos done similar things with the reported 24-pound bass he said he caught at the same lake, the bass fishing world would be a lot different right now.

The difference here is that Keznetzoff had all the documented proof of her catch. The difference is she had a very organized aunt in Signs, a woman who is focused on catching world-record fish. One of her BogaGrip scales goes to 120 pounds, "just in case I get a big flathead catfish," Signs said.

Signs finds it inconceivable that people like Trew and Duclos can fish for world records and then not follow all the IGFA's steps to document their catches for world-record consideration.

"If you're going to contend, you have to go by the rules," Signs said.

Keznetzoff, a freshman on the golf team at Granite Hills High, is no newcomer to fishing. She's been going to the Colorado River with her aunt since she was three years old.

"I remember her fishing for bluegill with her Snoopy rod

and reel," Signs said. "Once, as she was reeling in a bluegill, a bass came up and ate the bluegill."

Heather's best bass is an 8-pounder, and her aunt has cracked the 10-pound barrier for largemouth bass.

Signs was introduced to hunting and fishing by her late father, Phil. She feels his presence when fishing and has done everything she can to pass the traditions on to her niece.

"My dad would come by school and pick me up and take me fishing at the bay or one of the lakes," Signs said. "Whatever was on, he was there fishing for it. He loved it and passed that passion for it on to me. It just became part of my lifestyle after a while."

Signs took her father's early fishing lessons and turned them into a lifetime of adventure. She has caught 76 marlin, including a personal-best 320-pound blue marlin. She finished third in the women's Bisbee billfish tournament.

"I'd rather go to the tackle store than Nordstrom's," Signs said. "I fly to Florida just to go to the Bass Pro Shop and the IGFA Museum in Dania Beach."

Signs said she was considered a "tomboy" growing up, and now hears her niece say the same things.

"I hear it, too," Keznetzoff said.

They not only share an interest in fishing and hunting, but golf, too. Signs also surfs and rides a Harley-Davidson.

As a former road manager, Signs accompanied Paul and Linda McCartney on their World Tour. She worked McCartney's Rio de Janeiro concert in 1990 that drew an estimated 180,000 to 184,000 fans, still the world record for concert attendance. Signs filled a thick scrapbook of pictures from her World Tour experience.

These days, Signs fishes every chance she gets. She's off to the Colorado River this weekend, hoping to catch that record striped bass that has been eluding her.

Signs gladly gave the stage to her niece for her record, but knows her time will come. And if it doesn't, she'll have the reward of passing on her love of angling to her niece.

And it's refreshing to see this woman—someone who once escorted actor Jack Nicholson to Paul McCartney's backstage dressing room—get so excited and be so proud of her niece's 2-pound, 2-ounce bluegill.

My Old Man
and the Puget Sound

LOREN WEBSTER

I haven't fished for years for many reasons, not the least of which is that I tend to get violently seasick.

Still, reading Richard Hugo's poems recently reminded me just how important fishing has been to my life. My earliest, and most vivid, memories of my father are directly linked to fishing, probably the greatest joy of his life.

I was three or less when I started fishing with my father. I can still remember being dragged out of bed half asleep to make sure we were on the water at dawn when the fish were most likely to hit. I hated getting up that early, but it was worth the sacrifice to be out on the water with Dad, sometimes my mother, and my brother Bill. There are still some things worth getting up that early in the morning for, but not many.

I'm sure it would have been easier for Dad to leave us home

and go fishing with friends, but salmon fishing was a family ritual. Thinking back, I feel sorry for Dad, who had to spend the first thirty or forty minutes of fishing baiting Bill's and my hooks. I suspect, though, that I learned how to correctly bait a hook before I learned how to tie my shoelaces. But I wasn't allowed to bait my own hook, or at least drop it into the water, until I could do it correctly. I remembered this ritual years later when I read Hemingway's *The Old Man and the Sea*.

If you're going to be a successful fisherman, Dad taught, you do everything right. First, you find the best place to start fishing, no matter how far from the boathouse that might be. Lazy fishermen were willing to just drift for salmon, but not Dad. He would slowly row the boat while our lines were out, at least until we were able to afford a small motor to attach to the rented boat. Even at three you had to keep your line taut, not let the bait drift down too far. Few things are as embarrassing as bringing in a bottom fish when you're fishing for Kings.

There seemed to be as many rules to fishing as there are rules to life. When someone in the boat had a fish on the line, you always reeled your line in as fast as possible. Whenever someone else brought a fish in you complimented them on the catch, no matter how much you wanted to catch the biggest fish of the day. It was really, really hard to sound excited when you had the biggest fish going, especially when you're the littlest guy on the boat. And have no doubt that everyone, Dad included, wanted bragging rights to the biggest fish of the day. Bragging rights lasted until the next fishing trip.

Of course, sometimes you could be saved from the biggest fish put-down, because Dad would point out that certain kinds of salmon, though I was too little to tell the difference between anything but big and little, tasted better than others. And we weren't just fishing for fun. It was important to be recognized at dinner by someone saying, "This is the salmon Loren caught." We lived a good part of the year on those salmon and on the vegetables we had harvested from our garden. Whenever food became scarce, we always had salmon waiting in the freezer.

But most of all, I remember Dad's sheer enthusiasm for fishing. There are still vivid images of Dad standing up on the edge of the boat trying to net a huge salmon while Bill and I would desperately try to balance the boat by hanging out the opposite side of the boat, our combined ninety-five pounds no match for his two hundred pounds. "Don't rock the boat" has a very special meaning in the middle of Puget Sound for a four-year-old who can't swim.

Even when things had turned rough, yours truly had lost his breakfast over the side of the boat, the water would be breaking over the bow, the boat would be filling with water no matter how fast Bill and I bailed, and we would appear to be going backward, Dad would yell across the roar of the wind and water, "We're having a great time, aren't we?"

Strangely enough, we were.

My hiking partner has noted that when we get stuck in a precarious position—say six hours out on the trail, little or no food left, it's getting dark, and we're not quite sure where the hell we are or which trail to take to get us back before dark—that I always break into a laugh, a special laugh reserved just for such moments, a laugh that says I'm alive and having a great time.

That's when I know I'm Dad's son, even if I don't fish anymore because Dad isn't around to go with anymore and because I can't stand paying good money to throw up.

From *The Lobster Chronicles*

Linda Greenlaw

My father and I have fished together ever since I can remember. I was, in a way, my father's only son until my brother Charlie was born. And even after his birth in 1968, I stayed on as our dad's fishing (and hunting) buddy until Charlie, who eventually became Chuck, grew old enough to tag along and finally become the son when I outgrew the position. I was happy to have it again now that I was back and Chuck and his family were on the mainland. But it took Dad and me a while to regain ease in working together. Dad had learned that if he ignored 90 percent of what I had to say aboard the boat, we were both much happier. And 90 percent of what I have to say while hauling lobster traps is complaining about hauling lobster traps.

Each morning, as I climbed over the rail of the *Mattie Belle* to begin a day, I felt I had ample cause to complain.

The lack of lobsters began causing my disposition to sink to uncharted depths. My friend and former captain Alden would have given me grief about my mood, and we'd have ended up fighting. Dad just went about his onboard chores. Daydreaming became my escape. When I wasn't bemoaning my fate, I was imagining myself in another life. I fantasized about going back to offshore fishing. After all, my scheme to satiate my nesting instinct had failed. The admission that my plan to start a family had not been thoroughly thought out was taking a toll. I felt quite badly that I was getting increasingly hard to get along with, but couldn't seem to do anything about it. I could barely stand to be around myself. Unhappiness was something I had known so little of that I scarcely knew how to begin dealing with it. I had always been confident that I could achieve anything through hard work; the difficulty was only in deciding what I wanted to do. I had spent most of my life happily transiting from point A to point B to point C.... At this present stage, deciding on the next point of destination was agony. Maybe I would go to Alaska....

As the month progressed and August lurked, my daydreaming started to make me careless. One day, reaching into a trap, I felt a sharp twinge of pain race up my arm. In a jerk reflex, I pulled my hand out of the lobster trap to see what was causing the harrowing pain that started at the tip of my thumb. A large crab had clamped onto my finger and now dangled by a claw from my gloved right hand. "Ouch! You son of a bitch!" I flung both hand and crab toward the deck; the angry crustacean released its hold on contact. "Take that, you motherfucker!" I stomped the crab with the heel of my boot repeatedly, until it looked like it had been run over by a bus; I continued swearing with every stomp and grind. I had managed to flatten the shells and guts into a mass twice the crab's original diameter when I became acutely aware of my father's presence beside me.

My father seldom curses, and although he has never scolded me for it, I know he disapproves of the language I use aboard the *Mattie Belle*. I followed my father's stare from the dead crab to eye contact to the crab again and back to eye contact. "Wow, that hurt," I said.

Dad scowled and focused again on the dead crab. "I'll bet it did," he said quietly. It was much less from him than I wanted. In a move to gain sympathy, I pulled the glove off to inspect the thumb that was now pulsating between excruciating pain and dull ache. The nail was already purple and blood trickled from the cuticle. I assumed that my father would be concerned enough to examine the damage or at least indulge me with some words of condolence. But he was not and did not. I lowered my expectations to wishing that he would give me the satisfaction of telling me that I was a horse's ass. At least then I could argue with him and complain that *he* had not been the one bitten. But he did no such thing. Dad turned back to rebaiting the traps that rested on the rail, seemingly oblivious to the pain and humiliation I was suffering.

In one final act of frustration, I gave the Frisbeed crab a sound kick, sending it to the stern like a hockey puck. "Bastard!" I yelled, not knowing whether I referred to the crab or my father.

I had never hated lobstering more. Running the boat harder than normal, hauling faster than usual, and slamming things around in general, my anger slowly dissipated to self-pity with the hauling and setting of two strings of gear. Oddly, I soon became aware that I was gaily singing "King of the Road," and imagined my father might suspect me of being schizophrenic. Daydreaming always succeeds in pulling me out of self-induced emotional funks, and if I am singing, humming, or whistling, I am content within my own world. When I catch myself in the midst of a tune, I am never sure how many times I've repeated the same verse, but have been told by many a crewmember my repetitive singing is incredibly annoying. (I was once haunted by the chorus of "The Cover of the Rolling Stone" for a period of two weeks.) The singing I get from my mother. I knew every word to Petula Clark's "Downtown" well before I learned "Twinkle, Twinkle." Mom sings constantly when she's in the kitchen, which may be my connection between song and happiness, since my mother's cooking always makes me happy. "King of the Road" is still one of my old standbys; I was relieved to realize I was singing it while trying to escape the pain in my thumb and the reality of hauling largely empty traps.

In the midst of the third verse, I paused to yank a trap onto the rail and slide it aft to Dad, who waited for it. Another round of the chorus, and the second trap now rested in front of me. I opened the door and was delighted to find a feisty two-pound lobster. As I eased the lobster from the trap, I was disappointed to see that it was an egg-bearing female (egger)—back to the ocean with her. I turned with egger in hand toward my father, who was slipping by me with a freshly baited bag for my trap. A familiar voice on the VHF radio distracted me, and in an instant the egger had latched on to Dad's bare forearm with both claws. A lobster has two different and distinct claws—a "crusher" and a "ripper"—aptly named for their two separate functions, which they now performed on the white, sensitive underside of my father's arm, midway between wrist and elbow. She had both claws full of flesh and showed no sign of letting go.

I jumped out of the way to give my father room enough to swing the lobster against a bulkhead or splat her onto the deck as I had the crab. Dad stood patiently, supporting the weight of the lobster that hung on his left arm with his right hand. He was gritting his teeth, and he squinted as he waited for the lobster to relax and release. "Jesus, Dad. I'm sorry. She grabbed you so quickly. I wasn't paying attention." I felt terrible.

"Do you think you can gently pry her claws open?"

"Lay her on the rail." I was eager to help ease the pain I had caused. "I'll smash her for you." This offer was rejected with a disgusted sigh and a shake of his head. Pregnant female lobsters are always the most aggressive, but this one eventually released her ripper. I suspect she was thinking about getting a better grip, but before she could, Dad had the freed claw in his right hand, where he held it closed until she let go of him with her crusher. I tried to look at my father's arm, but he ignored me as he gently tossed the lobster into the water, being careful to land her on her back so as not to disturb the eggs on her belly.

"Bitchy female" was all Dad said. And as he returned to the bait bags, I wondered whether he was referring to the lobster or me. Assuming that "bitchy female" was referring only to the lobster, I defended her disposition, siding with the lobster in a male/female analysis that occupied my mind while my body performed what was necessary to finish the day's work. I had done a fair amount of reading pertaining to the biology of lobsters, and knowing that a female's gestation period can endure for up to twenty months, figured the egger had every reason to be bitchy.

As far as I can see, there is absolutely nothing attractive about a lobster, male or female, and I have often wondered how so many manage to reproduce. Obviously, lobsters find one another attractive enough to be remarkably prolific, although the mating rituals seem more perfunctory than romantic.

When the female lobster molts or sheds (loses her shell) she is as vulnerable as any girl who disrobes. Molting is triggered by water temperature and generally occurs around mid-July in the area I fish. (When I hear a radio report of "shedders in Duck Harbor," I can't be sure whether the fisherman has caught a soft-shelled lobster or spotted nude sunbathers on the shore.) The female lobster appears to dictate when the mating process will occur (not unlike humans, or so I'm told), for prior to molting she seduces the male out of his den with a squirt of pheromone that acts as a sexually stimulating perfume. The perfume, once emitted, attracts all male lobsters in the vicinity.

Levels of intelligence and bank accounts are not the criteria by which the female lobster judges suitable husbands. A lobster's prerequisites for paternity are simple and all physical. (How anyone has been able to determine this is beyond me. But this all seems to be common knowledge among those who have nothing better to do with their lives than study lobster sexuality.) From among the males she has enticed out of hiding, the female selects the one that is the largest and strongest. The exception being that Mother Nature does not permit lobsters to mate with siblings or first cousins. (No, not even in Maine.) Once she sets her sights on the stud, the female persuades him by sending his way a stream of urine loaded with pheromones. Intoxicated, the male advances aggressively with claws up. Depending on the nature of the particular female, she will either spar or turn away. Neither an overabundance of willingness nor being coy discourages the male, who is now quite persistent.

Eventually, the male lobster coaxes the female into his den, where they may remain for up to two weeks, waiting for the seductress to shed her shell. Once out of her shell, the female is in a state of precarious vulnerability, and the male must choose between two options: mate or eat. Voyeurs confirm that although the male may be quite hungry by now, he *usually* opts to mate with rather than consume his date. (I suspect that choosing between eating lobster and having sex would be more difficult for the human male.) The act itself, the experts report, is performed with "surprising tenderness." After mating, the female hangs around the den only until her new shell begins to harden a bit. Once protected with the new shell, she leaves her beau without so much as a backward glance.

While mating, sperm is deposited into a receptacle within the female's body that acts as a sperm bank. The female has the ability to store sperm for months, until her personal agenda permits pregnancy, at which time she fertilizes and lays her eggs. Lying on her back and cupping her tail, mother lobster pushes from her ovaries up to twenty thousand eggs that are fertilized as they leave the storage compartment. The fertilized eggs adhere to the underside of the female's tail, where they ride for nine to eleven months. The doting mother fans her eggs to keep them oxygenated and clean until the time comes to release them into the ocean, where they drift aimlessly with the current. Giving birth to twenty thousand eggs is quite a task and can take up to fourteen days.

It is estimated that, due mainly to predators, only ten of the twenty thousand released eggs will survive long enough to resemble what we think of as lobsters. After hatching from the egg, the lobster progresses through four larval metamorphic stages, developing into the strange creature that lobstermen refer to as a "bug." Drifting within a meter of the ocean's surface, larvae are easy prey for seabirds and fish until they drop to the ocean's floor in their fourth stage, between two and four weeks of age. Baby lobsters molt into a fifth stage, this time finding a place to hide for a period of up to four years. (It is tempting to suggest that certain children should try this.) During the time of hiding, lobsters venture out only to feed, and this only at night. Lobsters are nocturnal.

A lobster molts (which is how it grows) up to twenty-five times in its first five years of life. A newly molted lobster is somewhat fragile and extremely lethargic, an easy target for anything looking for a meal. Once an adult, the lobster molts once a year until it achieves maximum growth and maturity. A legal-sized and marketable lobster is approximately seven years old.

It seems quite clear that a female lobster spends the bulk of her life pregnant, molting, or hiding from predators. With a life like that, who wouldn't be a bitch? I wondered how the plight of the lobster could be stretched to somehow justify my own irritability of late, but abandoned the ridiculous effort as

we called it a day and headed for shore. Once ashore, I yelled to Dad that I would be home in time for dinner; he smiled and waved as he always does. His forearm was a mess where the lobster had grabbed him. I was aware that although I had whined about my thumb several times that day, my father hadn't mentioned his arm.

Father and Son Enjoy Creative Quality Time with Stripers

NELSON BRYANT

Aquinnah, Mass.—When we reached the top of the path through the dunes to Dogfish Bar a half hour before sunset, dozens of terns were diving into wind-ruffled Vineyard Sound a hundred yards to our right. Before my son, Jeff, and I reached the beach, we could see striped bass rolling on the surface, sometimes lunging half out of water in pursuit of their prey.

There were three other fishermen about a quarter-mile away and, so far as we could tell, they were not catching anything.

After fifteen minutes of tossing my fly—an imitation of a small sand eel—to breaking fish without a hit, I switched to a plastic-bodied floating fly with the same results. After that I tried a large, white squid fly. When it failed, I tied on a jet-black version of it that also produced nothing.

The sun went down, the terns departed and the bass continued their feeding rampage. I knew that they were dining on tiny sand eels because a few of those little fish, about an inch long and as big around as a large kitchen match, had been driven onto the strand by the voracious stripers.

Every June for the past three or four decades there has been a time when, for at least a week or so, the striped bass that have congregated along that beach, which is part of Martha's Vineyard Island's North Shore, refuse almost all offerings. It may have something to do with the many sand eels, a favorite food of the bass, that are present at that time. What are the chances of a striper's taking your imitation sand eel fly if it is swimming among thousands of the real thing?

That was why I tried the floating and squid flies. I was simply offering them something radically different, something that would stand out in the crowd.

"I haven't had a hit on my favorite striper fly," Jeff said. "I'm going to switch to a spinning rod and a jointed surface-swimming plug."

He got a hit on his second cast, and another on his third.

Wading over to me, he said, "They're taking at the very end of the cast, Dad, maybe sixty yards out."

That, of course, was far beyond fly-rod range.

A few minutes later he beached a fat striper about thirty inches long. An angler's daily bag limit in Massachusetts is two fish at least twenty-eight inches long.

He caught one more sublegal bass on that plug—I didn't get a single hit—before we called it quits.

I checked the stomach contents of Jeff's fish while filleting it: ten tiny sand eels and about three cups of sand and gravel.

This convinced me that at least one bass had been grubbing sand eels out of the bottom rather than pursuing their free-swimming brethren. When skin-diving, I have seen scores of sand eels facing upcurrent with their heads angled up out of the sandy bottom and more than half of their bodies buried.

So prompted, I tied up half a dozen weighted sand eel flies and began fishing one of those flies just above the bottom when Jeff and I got to Dogfish the next evening.

Once again, the terns were there, as were the sand eels and the bass. I used my fast-sinking fly for thirty minutes without a hit, then tried a floating fly for fifteen minutes more with iden-tical results. I went back to my original fly and, inexplicably, the bass found it attractive. I caught four bass in forty-five minutes, including one keeper that seized the fly in a burst of spray just as it hit the water. No bottom-grubber, she.

At one point, I was getting hits on every cast. Many of those strikes were little touches, and I knew the bass were grabbing the hookless tail end of the fly.

Jeff moved alongside.

"I guess you figured it out, Dad," he said. "I haven't had a hit."

I offered him one of my flies. He declined, saying that he was going to resort to spinning gear.

Soon, he was bringing fish ashore and releasing them. We caught fifteen fish between us that evening, keeping four that were over thirty inches. Clearly, the stripers had emerged from their persnickety eating habits.

Unable to resist the revitalized fishery, I was at Dogfish again the next night sans Jeff. It was a lovely evening in late June with a gentle southwest wind and a fast-flowing falling tide. It was nearly dark when I began casting, but not too dark for a pair of loons forty yards away to continue their fishing.

I immediately hooked a heavy fish on my sinking sand eel fly; five minutes later, it broke off. The leader had parted at the hook eye. I hadn't been heavy-handed, so I decided that I had simply fashioned a bad knot. I tied on another such fly, hooked another big striper—both fish went well into my backing on their initial runs—and was playing it with inordinate care when it also departed with my fly and part of my leader.

I backed up the beach and sat on a dunnage plank to better contemplate what was happening.

The answer finally came. I had tied up a new striper leader that day and had inadvertently used some old, deteriorated monofilament. I replaced the offending mono and immediately beached a thirty-two-inch fish, then hooked, played and released several slightly smaller bass in the next hour.

On my departure, the path through the dunes to my truck was marked by the white blooms of Rosa rugosa.

The Ties That Bind

From *We Fish*

JACK AND OMARI DANIEL

First Steps

Soon I was able to walk behind my father;
the rope would prod me along by
cutting into my sides
when it felt me falling too far behind.
I always hated the first step into the river.
When the water crept over my boots,
my buttocks clenched and shook violently.
I fell many times, the waters would wash over my soul
until my father pulled me up.

When I was eight, the cord was cut.
I was navigating the banks of the Juniata by myself.
My father's long strides would carry him away.

Finally, he would yell, and I would struggle to catch up.
I dreamed of being able to keep up.
A few years later, I could keep up for the first few hours,
but the pelting sun and the weight of my boots
made me drift further and further back.

At twenty, I am able to go stride for stride.
I am no longer a burden, but more of a friend, a competitor.
Every time I go back to those primordial waters,
I look at my reflection and realize
how far I have come.

It was really satisfying to see how independent Omari had become as a young man, how in some ways he was taking the lead as opposed to following me. One day, while wading in the middle of the river, I stopped to fish one of my favorite bass holes. Omari knew how much I liked the spot; it was one of those places on the river where I stood silently, enjoying the peacefulness of the water flowing by my waist, the hundreds of minnows darting around my legs, the two or three evergreens growing out the side of a reddish brown rocky hillside, the natural isolation of the area, and the occasional strike of a big fish. Though the first cast was usually his, Omari watched as I cast my line out, then continued wading toward a spot a few yards to my left. After about a half hour, I turned to tell him that it was time to move, but saw that he had waded about thirty yards away, where he was fighting a fish in a place we usually bypassed. The fish made a jump, and Omari began to take up the slack in his line as soon as the fish reentered the water. Slowly, he brought the fish in, took it off the hook, then gently released it like a veteran catch-and-release fisherman. Knowing that he had found the action, I waded to where he was standing in water deep enough to touch his elbows, and asked, "Why did you release that fish? My spot only got me a couple of baby bass. You're over here in water over your waist, letting nice ones go that we need for lunch today. What's going on?" He retrieved his bait, and moved a few steps so that I could get positioned for casting. Then, without looking at me, and in a somewhat instructional tone, he said, "This water is pretty deep. That fish hit before I could work my bait to the deepest water. I'm sure I can catch one or two nicer fish if I wade a little further. Like Uncle William always says, there's more where that one came from."

Instinctively, I was tempted to tell Omari to be careful as he inched into deeper water. Instead, I made a precise cast to a spot about ten yards in front of him. He simply smiled, seeming to know that I was quietly suggesting that he not wade into deeper water as opposed to poaching the area in front of him. Taking my hint, he took several steps to the side and made a cast longer than mine. An even larger smile appeared on his face when another of his casts was followed by the strike of a huge fish, just after I had made several more casts without getting a bite. Omari, too, had a lesson or two he wanted to teach, points he wanted to prove.

Later in the day, we met up with Henry Harris. As the three of us headed across some swift water, instead of the young child struggling to keep up with the older men, Omari's strong, athletic legs were easily outdistancing us. Looking back at me, he asked, "You need some help crossing through here? Be careful, this water's running real fast. You can hold on to my belt if you want." Not wanting to give credence to his last comment, I answered, "You go ahead. I'm fishing with Henry. We'll circle below and meet you down the river where that big sycamore tree hangs over the water."

Omari and I first began fishing the Juniata River the summer he completed kindergarten. Though he would never admit to being afraid, it was clear that he preferred not putting slimy wiggling night crawlers on his hooks. I wasn't sure of whether he was afraid of the worms, being stuck by the hooks, or both, but to save time and to avoid dealing with his emotional issues, I baited his hooks for him. Once while we were sitting on the bank, Omari dumped a worm on the ground, and attempted to stick it without his fingers touching it. The worm was especially lively, and after several minutes of watching this frustrating comedy, I put the thing on his hook, cast out into the current, and handed the rod to him.

During the early years, before we entered the river, I joined Omari to me with an eight-foot piece of rope that trainers use to lead racehorses. I tied an end of the rope securely around each of our waists, and it functioned as a safety line for him. Years earlier, my younger brother Stephen had been on the other end of that rope, and after Omari, my sister's son Daniel, and Stephen's son Bryan would take their places on the other end.

On first fishing trips, novices always proclaimed they didn't need to be tied to the rope, but after being in water up to their waists and having slipped a few times, the newcomers usually clung to it as a true lifeline. The first time I put the rope on Omari, he protested, "I don't need that rope tied to me. Last week, the lifeguard let me dive into the deep end of the pool and swim out."

"Yeah, but this river ain't no swimming pool, and I'm the lifeguard here."

"But you should have seen me. I dove into the deep about five times in a row. Nothing happened. So why do I need this rope on me?"

Before I could answer, he slipped, water came over his shoulders, the current spun him around, and I quickly used the rope to pull him to his feet. The rest of the day, as we waded, Omari held the rope tightly with both hands. When we stopped to fish, he was reluctant to let go and take his fishing rod.

Initially, when we got to the edge of the river and the rope was secured around our waists, I often had Omari climb up on my shoulders, to save time getting from one fishing spot to the next, and spare Omari the early morning wake-up calls from the cold water. With my child sitting on my shoulders, I carefully waded down the river's edge, holding our two fishing rods, and stopped several yards before a drop-off. Then I put him on the bank, I remained in the water, and we began to fish, allowing our bait to float downstream into the deeper water. Initially, fear of falling caused Omari's legs to lock around my shoulders, but by the third or fourth trip, he fortunately was no longer afraid, and I no longer felt like two miniature pythons were struggling on my back.

As I waded to large rocks on which Omari could safely sit or stand, I instructed, "Look at that dark-green water off to my left. The water is darker because it's deeper."

"How deep?"

"I don't know for sure, but it's over your head. If you cast slightly upstream and allow the bait to drift back downstream into that deeper water, you'll probably get one because the fish are sitting in there feeding. Let's stop and try it."

Using his rod, I made a cast above the deep water, and handed it to Omari. After he got a few nibbles and missed the fish by jerking his line too soon, I used my fingers to show him how fish often approach by quickly grabbing the bait and letting it go before they take the bait completely into their mouths. Then I cautioned, "So take your time. Let the fish run with it a bit, and when you see your line moving through the water, then set your hook by jerking up on your rod in the opposite direction from which the fish is swimming."

Although he usually listened or at least gave the appearance of listening, I'm sure he often hoped that I would shut up and just let him fish. Once something that I told him worked, however, he would repeat it over and over. I will never forget the twinkle in his eye the day we were sitting on the bank and I glanced over just in time to see him watching his line move through the water. He got up on one knee, expertly set the hook, and as I noticed his triumphant smile, I felt my own. When he could cast accurately for a good distance, I showed him how to cast far out into fast water, and to retrieve slowly until his bait reached the slower water. The first time that he tried this, a big channel catfish with a sagging belly pounced on his crab; to this day, he loves this maneuver, calling it the "Omari Retrieve."

Each year, each trip, each new stretch of the river, I let Omari wade a little more. When he slipped on the smooth sandstones of the riverbed and fell into water up to his neck, I quickly pulled him back up before the water could get in his face. It was very important that he not get frightened at an early age and get turned off to this form of fishing. As we crossed a swift current, in addition to the rope's support, I had him hold on to an extra belt I wore around my waist for his support, and I always kept him upstream so that I could scoop him up if he fell and the water began to carry him downstream. By the end of his grade-school years, I permitted him to extend the rope as far as it would stretch from me. I knew each spot I waded with him so well that I could navigate with the feel of my feet. This was especially helpful when the water was muddy, and I could test depths only by using my feet to feel for familiar landmarks.

For five or six years, it seemed as though I spent more time teaching him about the nature of the river, safety in the water and the woods, and the feeding habits of the fish than I actually spent fishing. Often, just as I was getting ready to do some serious fishing of my own, Omari needed help with things such as tying on a hook, baiting his hook, getting his hook off a snag, taking a fish off the hook, or unraveling his line which had formed a miniature bird's nest after one of his faulty casts. And my ultimate frustration came during those times when we had made our way through thick woods, gone a good distance across the river, and before we could fish, he pitifully informed me, "Daddy, I need to go sit on the toilet."

One day the fishing was poor, and Omari kept complaining about the heat and the May flies, though he had already sprayed enough insect repellant on himself that he glistened. I was regretting the fact that he was with me when, with the voice of a child's curiosity about something truly mysterious, he said very slowly and softly, "Daddy, something is pulling my line." Annoyed with both the flies and him, I said half angrily, "Don't tell me about something pulling your line. Set your hook! Set it now before the fish gets away!"

Standing there flabbergasted, he never did set his hook, and in the meantime, the hungry fish swallowed his bait and made a dash across the river. Now, he had the problem of bringing a large fish back across the current. However, as his rod remained bent downward, Omari confidently looked up at me and said, "I got him!" and added, "Looks like he is bigger than anything you caught today."

I put the fish on his stringer, and began casting to a likely place for fish to be holding. A few minutes later, Omari had another fish on the line, and he worked it for at least five minutes. I concentrated on working my bait through the water, pretending to be totally unconcerned with what he was doing. Finally, the fish was at his knees; it was clear that he would not be able to land the still-active fish while maintaining his balance in the water and fanning flies. I relented a bit.

"Lean against me while I take the fish off your hook. Keep your rod pointed up in the air, or the fish will get away. After I get this fish off, I'm going to put a crab on your hook because I think some big bass are in here."

Now oblivious to the mayflies, Omari shouted, "Hurry up! I want to get another one!"

"You're going to have to get another one."

Before he could ask why, I gave him a short glimpse of the huge rock bass, which I then dropped into the water. I wanted him to get over his fear of the flopping fish. As Omari stood speechless, I explained, "The sooner you learn to take the fish off your hook and put them on your stringer, the sooner you won't have to worry about me accidentally dropping one of your fish back into the river."

His sadness was short-lived, for as soon as I baited his hook, he made a long cast and waited intensely for another bite. In less than two minutes, he was complaining, "I thought that crab you put on was going to do so much." Irked by his comment, I explained, "If you'd just be patient and concentrate on what you're supposed to be doing, maybe you would catch a big one. Look, I've got a big one on now. He hit a crab, just like the one I gave you." While watching me, a big fish began to run with Omari's bait and he exclaimed, "I've got him!" His rod bent to the maximum and suddenly his line snapped. Returning to teaching him, I said, "You had him, huh? Hold your rod over here so that I can tie on another hook, and I'm going to give you one more of my good crabs."

About a dozen fish and thirty minutes later, I suggested it was time to move on to another spot. By now, his small body had adjusted to the water temperature. The flies all over his hat were no longer bothering him. Since I knew the water would become increasingly shallow as we approached the island we were headed for, I let him walk in order that he might gain additional wading experience. Preoccupied with what he had caught and what he might catch over on the island, he followed me on the rope, unconcerned with the fact that the water was considerably above his waist.

I was hard on Omari as I taught him to fish, but wading the river was very dangerous, and with one misstep, you could be in water over your head, weighted down by a stringer of fish, boots filled with water, and fishing tackle. I knew of two recent drownings, and the thought of something bad happening to my son was so overwhelming that I became compulsive with regard to making sure that he learned everything about wading safely, and still had fun. Part of my unwinding at the end of a fishing day consisted of being back at camp and reflecting on the fact that Omari was safe and sound.

One time the rope really did prove to be a lifeline. This particular day, after wading out into water over my waist, Omari got off my shoulders and sat on a huge rock. The water was just high enough to trickle over the rock, and so he had a seat as well as a form of natural air-conditioning. A few feet in front of the rock, the water was swift and more than six feet deep. After fishing for about fifteen minutes without a bite, we were wondering whether the long walk down to the spot had been worth the trouble. As I was scouting for the next place to fish, suddenly his rod bent over, and his line went sideways and upstream. As he fought the fish, its pull, the flowing water, and the slippery top of the rock combined to cause him to slide into the river. Except for the rope, the swift current would have swept him away in seconds.

His feet clearly were not touching the ground as he drifted into the current, and, dangling on the end of the rope, he reminded me of astronauts in space. Fortunately, he didn't tumble; his knee-high boots, full of water, helped to keep his feet down. The rope got tight. Neither of us spoke as I began to reel Omari in while he simultaneously pumped and reeled the bass like a pro, rather than a grade-school child. As he fought the fish, I gradually worked my way toward the riverbank, all the time using the rope to pull him closer to me. When he found himself in water shallow enough to plant his feet, he continued his fight with the fish, and I made a little slack in the rope to let him fight it on his own. This contest of fish, child, and rope affected me profoundly.

While Omari stood on the riverbank, admiring the huge bass wiggling slowly in the weeds at the river's edge, a tremendous sense of both terror and excitement overcame me. The flurry of events left me contemplating the possibility of losing Omari to the river, taking precedence over my reactions to him having caught the largest bass of his life (it was, indeed, one of the largest bass I had ever seen come out of this river). I flinched at my concern for the contest between the child and the fish over the safety of my son, and my mind was flooded with images; there were other times Omari had slipped and fallen into the water but I had not fully attended, I had simply pulled him up by the rope. Some of those times, the situations seemed funny and we had laughed them off, but now I wondered if any of them had really been funny at all.

My thoughts continued along this scary path; all of the times I had depended on the rope to rescue my son, I never thought about the possibility of the rope breaking or a knot failing. We both trusted the rope, and he trusted me so much that, when the trophy bass pulled him off the rock and into the deep, swift water, he continued to focus on the fish. I was overwhelmed by the extent to which Omari assumed that the rope and I were all the security he needed, and by the extent to which I had believed the same thing.

Omari's body slowly came into focus even though I had been staring at him all along. He was still standing there, admiring the fish, not realizing that no fish was worth risking his life. As much as I wanted him to learn from this incident, to talk about it, I was unable to speak, shaken by my own realizations and caught in the crosscurrents of fear, guilt, and excitement.

The rope incident continued to haunt me, and, throughout the rest of his childhood, I always kept an extra eye on Omari when we fished. Years later, I used my reading of "First Steps" as an opportunity to discuss with him the role of a metaphorical rope in the lives of the many African American children drowning in bad social circumstances. Returning from one fishing trip while he was a graduate student, I reflected back to the rope incident and pondered the terrible thing that could have happened. Then I reminded Omari of the situation, how the rope had saved him that day, and I asked him to tell me about the "ropes" in the lives of the inner-city African American children whom he taught during the summer. I was anxiously searching for ways to make meaning of our relationship for other African American males, and so I was really disturbed when he seemed to make light of my question by replying, "Tell you what? What is it that you don't understand? You're always making something big out of something obvious."

"You're the one who wrote about an umbilical cord. I never thought of the rope that way."

"Okay, now that you have, what do you make of it?"

I couldn't believe him. His analogy had sent me spiraling

into deep thoughts about complex African American male relationships. Since I was feverishly searching for answers and desperately wanted to know how he would extend his metaphor, I controlled myself. Calmly, I replied, "I've thought about it, but before I write anything, I want to know what you'd say about the ropes in these kids' lives." What he then said caused me to have a rush of excitement, and I took as many mental notes as possible while he held forth.

"First of all, some don't have any ropes and that's why they die young. For a lot of them, their supposed ropes are their gangs. Their gangs are supposed to save them from the bad currents in their lives. The gangs give them brother-to-brother and substitute-father relationships. If they're not in gangs, sometimes the rope for an eight- or nine-year-old is a relationship with a twelve- or thirteen-year-old brother or sister. But the trouble is that the person on the other end of that rope often doesn't know too much more than the young child does, or what the thirteen-year-old does know is something to get him and his little brother into all kinds of trouble, and maybe killed. And the people on the other end of these kids' ropes don't know as much about the streets as you know about the river, although they think they know everything about the streets. That's why so many of them end up dead, and you'd never let anyone drown. Those kids you're worried about might get killed by the very person who is supposed to be protecting them. And no matter what, they don't get the proper nourishment from their umbilical cords."

With that, Omari slumped into his seat and, as if to signal "end of discussion," pulled his hat over his eyes. I sped along silently, engaging thoughts about ways to develop strong ropes for African American men. It occurred to me that "ropes" might be rituals designed to acknowledge the different stages of African American males' growth and development, and that there had to be an extra-special ritual when they got off "the rope" and became men.

Now, as I was lying in my bunk quite pleased with the independence he had achieved, it was clear to me that, over the years, a young father had helped nourish a child to adulthood, a middle-aged father was now being nourished by his child. Signs of the changes flowed through my mind as I recalled a day on which, when we waded over to the bank, Omari quickly and effortlessly climbed out of the river and extended his hand to pull me up the riverbank. Then, too, responsibilities increasingly shifted to Omari as he began to do most of the driving once we got to the camp, and he determined where the best places were to fish on a given day. There is both self-respect and mutual respect for our acquired fishing skills.

Now, when we go fishing behind the school yard, I fish the riffles upstream, and Omari fishes the deep bass hole about fifty yards down. Despite the physical separation, I feel our connectedness and sense his moves and moods, as he casts, waits, sets the hook, looks slightly over his shoulder toward me to see if I have noticed, and reels in the fish. Like him, I tried to develop relationships with several other fishing buddies after Omari went away to college, but as is the case with him, fishing with others is "just fishing." Fishing together is affirmation. It came to me slowly, but finally I saw that the "together" was the most important part of fishing, and it was a pleasant and precious realization that, in the morning, we would get yet another chance to share the experience.

Hook Dreams

Long before Wayne Simien dreamed of basketball stardom, he developed a true passion to go fishing with his father

MICHAEL PEARCE

Leavenworth County—Wayne Simien's lead is slipping fast. A few moments earlier he'd been ahead 5 to 0, but the competition made two quick scores, narrowly missed a third and is playing and talking with more confidence.

Kansas's All-Big-12 forward responds to the run with his own taunts that come with smiles and laughs.

And sometimes the laughs are so long and loud, Simien has to regroup to get back to making the casts needed to stay in the fishing contest—the sport that came into his life before basketball.

"(Fishing's) always been there," he said. "It's in my blood."

And in Simien's case, "fishing" and "father" have always been synonymous.

Together Simien and his father, Wayne Sr., spent ninety short minutes of an early June evening in the old Ranger boat where fishing trips were once measured in hours and days.

"It's one of those rare times we can call our own," Wayne Jr. said as he fished. "Being outdoors is about our only time together."

Father and son fired cast after accurate cast into a private lake near Lawrence.

Wayne Jr. grabbed the early 5 to 0 lead, fast-retrieving a crankbait while his dad slowly finessed a plastic worm, hoping for a bigger bass.

A good-natured competition and ribbing came with the first cast.

When his dad tried to get a little credit for a big bass that had struck at his lure and gotten away, Wayne Jr. responded with, "I've missed some big shots . . . and they didn't count, either."

Wayne Jr. paused later and watched as his father cast from the shoreline, squeezing in every second of fishing.

"Look at him. He'd cast a Rat-L-Trap into a puddle of water," he said. "He can't help himself. He's got to fish."

So it's been in the family for at least five generations.

Being raised within this line of Simiens carries some solid traditions. You go to church. You study hard. You treat others with respect.

And you fish with your family.

As a boy, Wayne Sr. walked the shorelines of local ponds, rivers and creeks with his father.

His first paycheck as a manager-in-training at the Hallmark Cards plant in Leavenworth bought a car-top fishing boat. He fulfilled his longtime promise to "only marry a woman who could bait her own hook" with his marriage to his wife, Margaret. On dates, they fished for crappie and catfish all over eastern Kansas, then honeymooned on a bass trip to Missouri's Table Rock Lake.

Wayne Sr. said there was no question their son would share that joy of fishing.

"I had such a good time growing up fishing with my dad, I wanted to share those same things with my son," Wayne Sr. said. "I'd always looked forward to that."

Wayne Jr. was in a pint-sized life jacket and an infant carrier his first time aboard the family's fish-and-ski boat.

As soon as he was potty trained, son and father became almost inseparable on the water. The purchase of a top-of-the-line bass boat in 1989 took them afloat even more.

"A lot of my memories are in this boat," Wayne Jr. said as he started fishing, ". . . and they're all good."

Wayne Sr. used to carry his son, a fistful of G.I. Joes, and a sleeping bag to the boat.

"I must have grown three or four inches sleeping on that

crappie

boat seat," Wayne Jr. said. "Those waves would rock me to sleep. I'd wake up and mom had packed those big ol' lunches. It was quality time."

Before his first dribble in competitive basketball, Wayne Jr. had entered—and sometimes won—bass tournaments with his dad.

Wayne Jr. developed the soft touch needed to detect the whisper-light bite of a winter crappie. He mastered the complexities of a bait-casting reel.

But it was that precocious coordination, and his skyrocketing height, that increasingly tipped their time together toward basketball.

In 1994, Wayne Sr. had to sell a new Ranger boat he'd won at an Arkansas bass tournament—his best tournament prize—to buy the van that logged thousands of miles to basketball tournaments and camps.

Being a major college basketball player has limited Simien's fishing, though it's never far from his mind.

In the KU media guide, he listed Table Rock as his favorite vacation spot.

For his most memorable day, he listed a hot July evening when he outfished his dad and uncle.

"That's a championship for me," Wayne Jr. said.

On his neck, he usually wears a gold chain with a fishhook pendant that carries two meanings.

The gift from his father honors their mutual love for fishing.

A devout Christian, Wayne Jr. also sees it as a reminder to be a "fisher of men" by bringing others into his faith.

Father and son still make it to the lake occasionally, though in what some anglers consider not-worth-the-time lengths.

With two free hours before heading to the NCAA St. Louis Regional in March, they headed to Clinton Reservoir near Lawrence.

"I mainly fish Clinton on the outside chance Wayne can break away for even a little while," Wayne Sr. said. "I know our time together is getting shorter and shorter. I'll take an hour or whatever I can get and make the best of it. To be able to spend any time together is special to me."

That evening, they gladly took the ninety minutes and crammed in as much fishing, joking and reminiscing as possible.

When their time was over, Wayne Jr. sat a few extra minutes on a dock and talked of their past and their future.

Next summer, he expects to leave KU with a diploma and a solid shot at an NBA career.

With more time and money, he's hoping to live out his

boyhood dreams of fishing for things like Canadian pike and South American peacock bass.

He hopes to marry and have children. Being a Simien, he'll take them fishing at an early age. He'll also take his father.

"About the only guy I've ever really fished with is my pops," Wayne Jr. said softly. "I fished with (others). It felt awkward."

They'll also occasionally fish for Ozark bass and Kansas crappie.

But it won't be in the old Ranger on its third rebuilt motor—the only boat Wayne has known from first grade through college.

"When I go pro, he's getting a new boat," he said with a grin. "I've already told my dad that."

From *The Last Marlin*

FRED WAITZKIN

Baiting Fischbach

Abe's father, Joe Waitzkin, who lived in Cambridge, Massachusetts, was acidly critical of his son's lavish spending and murky business style. Where does it all go? Joe railed darkly in his thick Jewish accent. Abe spends the money before he earns it. For all his fancy jobs, one big building after the next, what money does he have to show for it? Joe complained about Abe's profligacy to whoever was around, to me and my mother whenever we visited, to members of his minyan in shul, but mostly to his daughter Celia, living upstairs with her husband Lennie and their three children in the same three-story house in Cambridge where Dad had been raised. As Abe's fixture sales reached dizzying heights, Joe's invective took on greater urgency, as though his son's way of life were violating the very essence of Judaism. And at the same time, "Pop," as we all called him, extolled I.R. as an American hero. During those years Pop earned his livelihood working in the Lee Products shop in nearby Everett that had been founded by Abe, an irony that did not escape my father.

As a younger man, a recent immigrant, Joe Waitzkin had been ambitious and hardworking and had accumulated considerable real estate in Cambridge. With the Depression he lost everything, and to my father's humiliation, Pop was forced to make a living in a corner grocery store. This big failure left Pop a frustrated and angry man. I recall one afternoon when the Lee shop was in the midst of moving from one location to another. I happened to be standing in the doorway while Lennie and a few workers were dismantling the dingy office. My grandfather began striking the unyielding timbers of the wall with a hammer. He struck blow after blow as though trying to slay an enemy. This went on for what seemed like a long time with Pop sweating and Lennie and the others begging him to stop. He beat the wall until he was doubled over and heaving.

Even during Pop's calmest moments I found it difficult to pierce his simmering rage and religious fervor to have a proper conversation with him. I cannot remember ever seeing my father and his dad together when there wasn't anger. I wonder if Pop ever paused to consider that his own fall from success contributed to this son's unremitting drive to reach the top, to live rich. On the other side Dad complained to me that Joe and Lennie operated the business in Everett like a mom-and-pop store, kept no inventory because of the financial risk and had no plan or ambition to expand. All they wanted from Lee, Dad would say, was a modest weekly income. With all the big deals in New York, Dad had little time to focus on expanding the Everett shop, which employed only six or seven men who labored on out-of-date presses and lathes. Still, the timidity of his family was frustrating to my father, who would have liked to send them large orders from New York contractors he had befriended.

Dad's sister Celia was caught in the middle of warring sensibilities, titillated by her brother's flair and success and yet mindful of both the wrath and reproach of her father and the more conservative business approach of her husband, who ran the Everett shop. Probably because my mother couldn't have cared less about Abe's wheeling and dealing, Dad frequently called Celia in Cambridge with stories about the union guys he courted, what clubs they went to and such. In the Great Neck house, Dad talked on the phone to his sister with the door closed, and it made me jealous that he told Celia secrets he kept from me.

My smart, chesty aunt glowed in Abe's presence and at the names of the great men who never kept him waiting, like Charlie Zweifel, another electrical contractor, not to mention Alan Fischbach himself, who would soon take over the presidency of the enormous Fischbach and Moore. Dad and I often visited Cambridge. As the family sat around the kitchen table chewing salad with Kraft French dressing, Celia chose the best slices of steak for Abe, turned them lovingly on a counter rotisserie until they were perfectly well done, the way her brother enjoyed his meat. She served Abe first, while the rest of us waited for our steak. Later, when the kids were in bed, Celia stayed up until two in the morning eating ice cream and talking with her brother about his newest deals. Between them was the tacit promise that Abe's skyrocketing prosperity would spread north to Cambridge and Everett, the Lee shop would someday swell with Charlie Zweifel and Fischbach deals. There was no need for formal agreements between these two. In a world of sharks Abe trusted his sister completely. Within the pull of their intimacy, I felt like an intruder.

Whenever Celia tilted too far in her brother's direction, her husband, Lennie, became irritated—why was Abe such a big deal? After all, Lennie had also bought a boat, a little lapstrake, and trolled daisy chains of squid off Magnolia on summer weekends. Why do you cook the best pieces of meat for Abe? But then, Celia had ways of making it up to Lennie, and he worshiped her.

One time Dad brought Alan Fischbach to Celia's summer cottage in Magnolia. "Alan loved Abe," recalls Celia. "The day he came I accidentally locked myself out of the house. Alan was very tall, six feet four, but he crawled through the bedroom window to unlock the door. The sheets were messy but Alan didn't mind." Celia titters over this incident forty years later, as though the king of England had crawled across her messed-up sheets.

Needless to say, I shared my father's view that Pop's criticism of our spending habits was small-minded. True, Dad was often short of cash, but who lived like him, like us? I adored my father for all the great restaurants and fancy trips, for never settling for less than ringside or box seats behind home plate. And no mistake about it, we were getting ahead, closing in on the forty-footer. Together we searched through boating magazines and debated the pros and cons of Huckinses, Wheelers and Rybovichs—the gold platters of the sportfishing world. Each of Dad's trips edged us closer.

I was incomplete when he was away. I treaded water until he was back and we could count his successes over our breakfast cereal and make our plans. On one trip Dad took a couple of union guys down to Puerto Rico for several days of marlin fishing. For some reason he wouldn't take me along, and I was beside myself when he left. He rarely fished without me and such was our camaraderie on the ocean that it was hard for me to believe he would leave me behind. I paced the halls of Great Neck High wondering about their trolling. For three days I could think of nothing else but Dad's lines slipping through the ocean.

He arrived home at two A.M., after I had fallen asleep. In the morning I could hear him snoring in his bed. I was bitter for not having stayed up for him as I had intended, for having squandered an opportunity to talk about his adventure off San Juan. I could barely contain myself while Dad spent twenty minutes in the bathroom. I knew this time was painful for him as I sometimes heard him moan on the toilet.

Finally we were in the kitchen together. Winnie the maid poured Cream of Wheat into our bowls. "How'd you do?" I tried to ask with a measure of detachment. Dad was beaming. "I caught a marlin." A blue marlin! How had he ever managed it? I didn't think my father had the physical strength to pull on such a fish. I quickly concluded that it must have been a small one, but I didn't make him tell me this. According to Dad's narration, the fight was easy except for the sharks. Soon after he had hooked the marlin three or four big bull sharks circled the boat, attracted by the struggling fish's blood. But the captain knew what to do. He took twenty feet of wire leader and twisted large hooks on both ends. Then he put a mullet on each hook and tossed the rig over. In seconds the baits were grabbed by two large sharks. Dad and the union guys could see the roiling on the surface as the sharks twisted and smashed their tails trying to get free of each other. After throwing over several of these rigs there were no more sharks, and Dad was able to wind in the marlin.

The Last Marlin

At the funerals of family members and beloved pets, my brother stepped forward, made sharp decisions and showed an attention to detail not generally apparent in his daily life. I think at such times the past came alive for Bill and he felt a calling and responsibility. He had long been fascinated by the pharaohs and had studied the *Book of the Dead*. He believed in a connection between the meticulous preparation of the grave site and some form of eternal life. While I was spooked and tentative around my father's death, it was my brother who selected Abe's coffin. He knew what color and style were best for Dad, what shaped pillow and what little objects—pliers, pen, writing pad, cigarette lighter—to place in the pockets of his business suit, and which suit, which little shoes would travel with Dad through all of time.

And now weeks after Abe's death, Celia, Bill and I were seated in a cramped office with two dusty desks piled high with notebooks, directories and old stencils. On the plate-glass window was a sign that read, SAM CANTER & SONS, ARTISTIC GRANITE MONUMENTS.

My aunt's face was puffy and red. It's not fair, she said, wiping her eyes.

Sam Canter, a portly man, nodded to her in a caring manner. Sam understood the slow and intractable rhythms of grief. He had walked with a thousand customers down this path.

My brother was wearing the pants from one of Dad's old suits, his stomach bulging over the top, and his beard was full, his bushy hair brushed back for the occasion and held in place with a rubber band.

You know, you look like a rabbi, my aunt said, trying to smile. She used to say that to calm my father down when he was incensed about Bill's appearance and incomprehensible life choices.

Sam was very smooth and we hardly noticed when he brought out the big and shiny book of possibilities. There were gray and red gravestones, one big black one, an imposing stone. That one is rarely used, he said in such a way as to imply an impropriety. My aunt shook her head decisively, never, never that one. But size really wasn't an issue. The stone would be the same height and gray color as those to the left and right, his father and cousin. We wouldn't want to make it look like he was a king, right? she asked Sam Canter, who nodded and paused a beat.

The big thing, he explained, is whether to choose the polished or the natural surface and whether you want the top of the stone straight horizontal cut or one of several sloping curves and the kind of border you want, which depends completely on whether you choose polished or natural and, of course, the wording of the stone itself. But the big decision would be between the natural or polished stone: that's what determines the lettering technique and the border, Sam repeated.

It was a confusing and painful choice made more difficult by the plastic page coverings that protected Sam's photographs from rough handling but made it difficult to tell the difference between natural and polished.

After some time we decided that the polished was best for Abe. Then Sam pulled out his drawing pad in order to sketch out a few stones. Should we keep it simple? he asked, drawing with dexterity. Usually it's the Hebrew name over the American, although we can do it the other way. What is the Hebrew name? he inquired looking up from his sketch. Avram, my aunt said tentatively.

Sam nodded and took a solemn breath. Avram above Abraham, he continued. Then comes the dates below the names; or you can have it the other way around, put Abraham over Avram. Sam was sketching it both ways, so we could make a considered decision, when my brother spoke up.

I'd like to put a fish at the top of the stone.

A fish?

Well no, not just a fish. A blue marlin. That's a very special game fish.

Celia stretched her skirt lower on her legs. She had been hoping this idea would go away.

It might be wrong, she said emotionally.

Is this fish on a line?

No, it's free. In the evening when the sun is setting, marlin sometimes jump like this. No one knows why they do it. I want the marlin leaping off the top of the stone. I'll draw the fish. And you make a stencil from my drawing. Just like these stencils of flowers here on your desk. Except this will be a leaping marlin. That's it.

Was your father in the fishing business? Sam asked, absorbing a new wrinkle in an old business.

No, my father was in the electrical business.

Sam shrugged.

Are you sure there's nothing wrong with it? my aunt asked. Nothing in the Jewish Law which says we shouldn't?

Sam seemed to be searching through the Jewish Law for the answer.

I don't know anything in the Jewish Law which says we can't put a marlin on the stone.

Are you sure, Sam? she pressed him.

There is one thing. You people decided on the polished stone. But with this fish we'll have to cut it on the natural.

Later that night Bill drew the blue marlin. It was a simple outline of a stout jumping fish that looked remarkably similar to marlin he began drawing as a kid in Great Neck on his school assignments. My brother had dragged the marlin of his childhood across the years and put it more or less unchanged onto the margins of his favorite books, like *Madame Bovary* and *Gone with the Wind*, and on the pages of rough drafts of his magazine profiles of afternoon soap stars. He also put them at the bottoms of postcards from distant places to me and Dad, like a signature. To the best of my knowledge my brother stopped sketching this frisky, guileless marlin after the one he gave to Sam Canter for Dad's stone.

A Father Has His Final Fishing Wish Granted

Marc Folco

George Horn's wish—and more importantly, his will—was to be able to make it to his annual fall salmon-fishing trip to the Salmon River in Pulaski, New York.

It's a trip he enjoyed with his two sons, George and Russell, for the past fifteen years. Their tight-knit group included another nine anglers, many of whom are relatives and close friends. Every year, they'd get together for the fall run of cohos, kings and Chinooks, which has made the river famous as a trophy salmon fishery.

coho salmon

The Horns were a rugged trio of outdoorsmen who fished together since the boys were toddlers and hunted together since they were teenagers. The senior George, sixty-four, lived in New Bedford, but was born and raised in New York's Catskill Mountains. He was a large, jovial man, about six feet three inches tall, strong as an ox, and his sons are younger carbon copies of him.

For George, life's treasures were simple pleasures—family, joking, laughing, cooking, eating, hunting and fishing. He enjoyed cooking so much that he used to get involved in New Bedford's Men Who Cook event, and ran the Christmas dinners and other suppers at the Fin, Fur and Feather Club of Mattapoisett for many years, where he was a long-time member.

In April, he underwent quadruple bypass surgery without a hitch. He had retired from the Massachusetts Department of Correction, then worked in the maintenance department at Hawthorne Medical and at the Truesdale Clinic.

Within six weeks of his open-heart surgery, he was back to work at the clinic, cracking jokes like he always did. Shortly after however, in mid-June, George and his family were dealt a devastating blow.

He was diagnosed with a malignant brain tumor.

He endured surgery and radiation treatments, but the sad news was that it would only prolong his life, not save it. The illness was terminal.

Throughout his ordeal, all he wanted to do was go on that fishing trip.

"That's all he talked about," said Russell, who lives in Fairhaven. "After his surgeries, before he regained his speech, he'd be in the hospital bed and when we asked him if there was anything he wanted or needed, he'd make casting and reeling motions with his hands.

"Dad's neurosurgeon, Dr. Phillips, and his assistant, Mark White, both fish, so they took to my father right from the start and a bond was struck. It's a bond that I think only out-doorspeople know. After one of Dad's surgeries, he gave my mother hand signals on what he wanted her to do."

George's wife, Maureen, understood exactly what he meant. Using simple hand gestures, he told her he wanted her to bring him a particular box of flies that he had hand-tied himself. The box was on a certain shelf in the garage.

Maureen brought it back to the hospital and George picked out some flies to give to Dr. Matthew Phillips and PA Mark White.

"It was a kind, generous and heartwarming gesture, and they're beautiful," Dr. Phillips said. "They're almost too nice to use, but it would be a shame not to, so I took one bass fishing with me the other day."

As George continued to fight for every precious minute, his hopes were high that he'd be on the Salmon River at the end of September, but in reality, the outlook was bleak. His family prayed that he'd make it, but he was taking a turn for the worse. The brain tumor began causing blood clots through-out his body. A week before they were scheduled to leave, he began lapsing into a coma. A cyst on his brain was expanding and emergency surgery was performed to drain it on a Friday. On Monday, another surgery was performed to remove it.

When he was recovering shortly after coming out of the operating room, the nurses were worried about him because he was having difficulty following commands. So Dr. Phillips got a fishing picture of himself holding up a big bass. He woke George up and as his eyes fluttered open, he showed him the picture.

"He gave me a big smile and a thumbs-up," said the doctor. "I told the nurses he was going to be alright."

Not only had he struck a bond with the doctors, but with the nurses as well. It was George's kind, jovial nature that warmed their hearts also.

He soon was making the nurses laugh again. They knew how much he loved fishing and found a scrub hat for him, with flies on it. George was released on Wednesday, September 24, just two days after brain surgery and two days before they were supposed to leave for their trip.

"We never thought Dad would be able to go," Russell said. "He was just barely getting around with a walker. My brother and I decided we weren't going either, with Dad just getting out of the hospital. We were going to cancel out, but he still had his heart set on it. We didn't know what to do, then Dr. Phillips told us that he could go. He should go. He said, 'However you can, get him there.'"

"So my sister, Jodi (the youngest of George's three children) starting cooking," Russell said. "She's the baker in the family and always made a bunch of stuff for us to bring on our fishing and hunting trips. One thing Dad never lost was his appetite. We borrowed a wheelchair so he'd be able to get around easier and got the rest of the gear ready."

The plan was to leave Friday at noon, "But Dad called the house at six in the morning and said he was ready to go—he was sitting in the garage with his gear," said Russell's wife, Joyce.

"Dad was always ready to go hunting or fishing long before we were supposed to leave," Russell said. "He was always at the kitchen table, playing with his flies and tackle and he'd have his stuff packed and organized in the garage a month ahead of time."

They brought Mohammed to the mountain and made the journey to Pulaski.

Saturday morning, on the banks of the Salmon River, George donned his chest waders and readied his tackle. They had to climb down a steep, rocky bank, and the brothers agreed that getting their father down wouldn't be as hard as getting him back up.

Russell said, "The important thing was getting him down there. We said we'd worry about getting him back up later."

George sat in the wheelchair with his tackle box on his lap, fishing rod in his hand, and his two big, strong sons eased their father down the bank. Instead of sitting him high and dry on the bank, they wheeled him into the river and he sat shin-deep in the current, so he was fishing alongside the other anglers. It was the next-best thing to standing in the river in waders.

"Dad was so happy, he couldn't stop smiling," Russell said.

He was reveling in the camaraderie among their group—the joking, laughing, fishing and eating. All things he loved to do. And he was happy to see the old friends they had made on the river. They were anglers that they had seen at least a dozen years out of the past fifteen that they've been going.

"The guys were almost always there the same weekend we were, so we got to be good friends," Russell said. "Dad always looked forward to seeing his buddies."

George, who had limited mobility on one side because of the surgery, landed a nice coho salmon with a little help from his sons. And it truly was a remarkable trophy.

"Boy, was he happy to see that fish come in," Russell said.

At day's end, George and Russell carried their father back up the steep, rocky bank.

To use a cliché: he wasn't heavy, he was their father.

George had carried his sons proudly up and down banks of rivers and ponds to go fishing when they were boys, and now the roles were reversed.

On Sunday, George didn't land a fish, but he continued to bask in the ambiance on this warm, sunny, autumn day. "He still had that smile on his face the entire time and he was happy to see us all catch fish," Russell said. "He didn't like to come home empty-handed. He always had people back home who he had promised to bring salmon back for."

George's health was improving by the hour. He was getting stronger. He was talking better. And on that afternoon, instead of being carried, he walked back up the bank, flanked by his sons, an arm around a shoulder of each.

The weather turned stormy overnight, and Monday morning was met with thunder and lightning. They headed home, stopping every forty-five minutes so George could walk and circulate the blood in his legs.

"We called Mom often every day because she was worried about Dad and on the way home, I told her, 'He's doing great. He's just like his old self again.'"

They pulled into the driveway and Russell helped his father out of the truck, but George collapsed in the driveway before he got in the house. They called an ambulance and he was rushed to the hospital.

A blood clot had traveled to his heart and more went to his lungs. He was nearing the end of his line.

His physical strength reserves kept him alive for more than a week with his family by his side around the clock.

This past Tuesday, Russell and Joyce shared the family patriarch's story and also some pictures of that grand fishing trip and from hunting and fishing trips past. They were sad that the end was near, but Russell said that he thanked God his father made it to the Salmon River one last time.

Then tears welled up in his eyes and he said, "He was my fishing and hunting buddy." And he began to cry.

George died Wednesday afternoon, a rich and contented man.

"I feel honored to have met George and his family," Dr. Phillips said. "They are the people who reconfirmed my belief in humanity. When you read about all the terrible things people do in this world, you sometimes say, 'Why bother?' Then you hang out with the Horns for a little while and realize why.

"George was a guy who was 'alive.' He was a very strong man and his inner strength and strong will were just an extension of his physical strength. He lived every second. And his family has the same outlook on life. To see someone who can continue 'living' when faced with a terminal illness is inspiring.

"George's death is tragic, but at the same time, it seems to make life that much more important. He certainly leaves a legacy in more than one way."

A Wish Come True

ROGER LEE BROWN

A few weeks ago in the late afternoon while I was re-spooling one of my fishing reels, my wife yelled down to me in the cellar and said that I had a phone call.

I asked her who was on the phone, to which she responded, "I think you'd better get this call." So I stopped what I was doing and picked up the phone.

The voice on the other end of the phone introduced herself as Cheryl from the Make-A-Wish Foundation. She then proceeded to ask me if I was the Bass Coach (I own a fishing school and bass charter service in upstate New York), to which I responded in the affirmative. Cheryl then told me that a seventeen-year-old boy by the name of Jared who resided in Michigan had made a wish.

Now, I had heard of the Make-A-Wish Foundation in the

past and even donated to it, but I wasn't sure how the foundation really functioned; I just knew that they helped people with terminal illnesses make their wishes come true. Cheryl told me that Jared, who had leukemia, had specifically requested to meet me in person, and that he wanted me to teach him how to fish for bass. I was speechless, thinking how honored I felt.

The Make-A-Wish Foundation and I set up a time slot that was open on my calendar and scheduled Jared and his father to attend my bass-fishing school. Much to my surprise, the foundation made it possible for Jared's whole family to come along with them. When the first day of the school came, I picked up Jared and his father, Ron, at the bed-and-breakfast where they were staying. The first impression I got from Jared was a good one. He was a tall, slim, good-looking boy with a great personality. The three days went quickly, and after spending time with Jared and his father I couldn't help but get attached to them. We had so much fun fishing together; I enjoyed just being able to teach them how to use different baits they'd never used before and consistently catching bass with them.

Jared told me that he used to fish with his grandfather off and on through the years while growing up, but now his father had a chance to learn not only how to catch bass, but how to spend more quality time with his son, fishing together as a family should. During those three days, Jared and his father not only learned how to fish for bass; they learned how to enjoy just spending time together, doing something they now had in common.

When the last day approached I felt profound sorrow for Jared because I knew that I probably wouldn't have a chance to see him again. In the little time that I had spent with him, I found him to be an amazing boy with a positive attitude toward just about everything that he talked about. I don't know how most of us would react if we were in Jared's situation, but I do know now what strength, love, caring, and having friends and family is all about. I know the Lord has reasons for everything that He does, and I'm sure that he had a reason for Jared's condition, but I would gladly trade places with him if I could. I just want Jared and his father to know that I'll always hold a place in my heart for them.

Passing on Love of Fishing
from Father to Son
to Grandson

DAN DURBIN

Johnny Cash played softly as my father, Phil, son, Hunter, and I motored down Highway VV on our way to Lake Keesus in Merton.

As we drove, I pictured my dad and his father, Eli, listening to Cash on their old pickup on the way to a Tennessee lake somewhere.

They didn't have a CD player in the truck back then, but Cash just seems to go with the ambiance of a first fishing trip.

It was my three-year-old son's first real fishing trip, and what better way to share it than with my own father on Father's Day weekend?

Like many fathers and sons, Dad and I communicate best

when on a fishing or hunting trip. Sometimes it's between casts. Other times it's over a crock of chili back at the shack.

As we got to the launch, I heard my wife, Lisa, in my mind: "Make sure he has his life preserver on right," she said. "Don't let him get too close to the side of the boat. Put plenty of sunscreen on him."

She might as well have asked me not to let Hunter eat the worms we were using as bait. Or, don't let Hunter jump in the livewell and use it as a bathtub. I mean, come on: I might not have been in all the advanced courses throughout school but I'm not exactly on the intellectual scale of a roach either.

She means well. Always does, as any mother should.

After backing the boat down and getting her off the rack, Dad asked where we were going to fish, as a courtesy really, because he knows where fish lurk.

This was pretty new to me. Most of my life, I always asked Dad where we were going to fish. Or, as a kid, begged him to fish in certain areas because we had luck in those spots in the past or I just thought they looked cool.

Most of the time, when I was young the spots I wanted to fish never panned out.

Maybe he let me fish those spots to educate me. Sooner or later, I figured out that the fish just don't hang out on "pretty" sandy areas much.

While cruising out to our first spot, we went over some rules for Hunter.

"Be careful," Dad said. "And don't touch the hooks or they'll get ya."

I remember the first major rule of fishing engagement that I broke. We were in Minnesota on a family vacation. There were probably close to twenty relatives at the resort. We were on a lake, and each day I was the first one up casting off the pier for bluegills and bass.

"Make sure that no one is behind you when you cast," Dad said. "These docks are small, and there are a lot of people with us. You don't want to hook anyone."

Yeah, sure, Dad, I thought. Me and my ten-some years of life knew what I was doing.

After a packed family pontoon boat ride, we eased up to the dock, people beginning to exit the craft. Just then, a huge fish rolled off the end of the pier, and I was off and running. I picked up my rod and fired out a cast with all of my adolescent might. My cast stopped mid-arch, however, and the Minnesota calm erupted with a loud: "STOP!"

I had put the business end of a hook deep into my Uncle Rick's finger and nearly pulled him off the dock.

Luckily, Hunter didn't hook anyone.

The key to introducing a three-year-old to fishing is keeping the action fast—and it was.

"Oh, oh, oh," Hunter said. "It's a big one, Papa Phil."

A bluegill all of four inches nearly had itself reeled into the end-guide of the rod, as Hunter wasn't about to let the monster get off. About thirty fish later, with some actual decent crappies really testing out Hunter's ultra-light rod, we headed back toward the dock.

Now I can't wait for my fourteen-day-old son Blake to take his first trip a few years from now, with Papa Phil showing him the ropes.

white crappie

Judge, He Was Delicious

From *Fishing by Mail*

Vance and Philip Bourjaily

Brunswick, ME

Dear Philip,

This is a long way from my little red house in Baton Rouge, in the vicinity of which freshwater fishermen sit at anchor watching bobbers, beneath which dangle split-shot and hooks baited with crickets. When a 6-inch bream is caught, there is satisfaction, if not exhilaration. Uncatchable mullet flip exuberantly in and out of the water, and inedible gar rise to the surface to sun themselves. There are said to be good bass lurking around the cypress knees, which I don't doubt, but the exciting fishing is in the salt water of the Gulf, an hour away, for redfish, snapper, and speckled trout, and for big-game fish farther out.

Here in Maine, fresh water is something else. John Yount came by yesterday to eat a decent number of lobsters and invited me to join him and Art DeMambro on what sounds like a rather scary fishing trip for landlocked salmon. The west branch of the Penobscot, where they're going, is a river that draws more whitewater nuts than fishermen. Those who wade do so cautiously. John and Art are taking a canoe, with a small motor, a big anchor, and John's considerable experience from his own whitewater feats.

"Love to go," I said with my best weasel smile. "But don't worry about making room for me in the boat. I'll just fish from shore." I believe John chuckled.

We didn't talk much about the fish, of which I know nothing. Tomorrow I shall do some angling at the Bowdoin College library, though I'm aware of the ancient wisdom that says you can fill your creel with facts but you can't sauté them *amandine*.

Love,
Dad

Homestead, IA

Dear Dad,

Glad you're going on another fishing trip. You haven't done enough of that in the last few years. But why you would leave the safety of your polluted, gator-and-cottonmouth-infested Louisiana bayous to go fishing with John Yount, of all people, is beyond me. Remember, it was John's whitewater-canoeing partners who, as Yount legend has it, waited until he was safely aboard the plane home before they fell to their knees and kissed the tarmac chorusing, "He's gone, he's gone, and we're still alive."

The last time you and I went fishing with John—and it must have been about 1971—he took us on a whirlwind tour of northeast New Hampshire during which time I fell into three of a possible four rivers in the space of three days. The biggest and whitest-watered of these was the Androscoggin, which John himself admitted was "pretty rough," although he also promised it held trout "as big as your leg." I don't recall seeing too many leg-sized trout as I bounced around the bottom, but it certainly was wet and cold down there.

Incidentally, the Androscoggin flows into the Atlantic right near Harpswell. If you get a chance you might check with the Coast Guard and see if they ever picked up any of my stuff.

Love,
Philip

Brunswick, ME

Dear Philip,

My best fishing buddies in the dark waters of the Bowdoin library were Byron Dalrymple, Derek Mills, W. B. Scott, and a man with a perfect name, Anthony Netboy. From their works the following is cheerfully plagiarized. Landlocked salmon are a non-migratory form of *Salmo salar*, the Atlantic salmon. People used to think there were two distinct kinds of landlocks—the sebago and the ouananiche—and each kind was classified as a separate subspecies of the Atlantic. Today we've pretty much decided such distinctions were over subtle; all Atlantic salmon, migratory or no, are now tossed into the same taxonomic pot.

Exactly how landlocks get landlocked is open to question. Some may have been trapped in fresh water when their river systems were rearranged by glaciation. Others, however, have a clear shot at the sea but don't take it. The closest that men ever came to establishing Atlantic salmon in the Pacific was at Lake Te Anau in New Zealand. The fish crossed them up. They had access to the ocean, but chose freshwater life and were doing fine until the introduction of brown and rainbow trout; the salmon are very scarce now.

In Lake Ontario, which, in 1835, had an enormous population of landlocks, they aren't just scarce, they're extinct. On the Canadian side it's claimed that someone once landed a 44-pounder. Our North American landlocks, living principally in Maine and eastern Canada, have analogues in Sweden, Norway, Yugoslavia, and Russia. If you happen to be fishing in Sweden, just ask the folks around Lake Vänern what's the hot fly for *blanklax*.

Lake Sebago, Maine, is where the unofficial U.S. record fish was caught, back in 1907. It went 22 pounds 8 ounces, and I'm not at all sure I want one anywhere near that size on my line two weeks from now, dragging John's canoe toward the rapids.

That name "ouananiche," by the way, is an Indian word meaning "he drowns you in the water and laughs like crazy."

Sea-run Atlantic salmon are fished for on their spawning run, when they aren't feeding, and no one understands why they take flies at all. But landlocks are easier to catch because they feed year-round, my authors say they readily take flies, spinning lures, and various trolled baits, probably including live goats. When they can't get goat, smelt is their favorite food—landlocked smelt, actually—so that streamer flies like the Gray Ghost are recommended.

I'm advised that the best fishing is just after ice-out and again in September, neither of which corresponds to late May. I'm also advised that landlocked salmon hunt their food in rough water, as if I needed to be reminded.

But my next fishing place will be L.L. Bean, which should be relatively safe and a lot of fun. I'm to meet Art there on the way to the river.

Love,
Dad

Homestead, IA

Dear Dad,

You think a visit to L.L. Bean is safe? Ask the next guy you see sleeping on a park bench under a pile of old Herter's catalogs. Chances are the last thing he remembers is going into Bean's tackle department to buy some leaders. Just thinking about the place makes me want to spend money I don't have. If you see anything I need, like a couple of popping bugs or a 16-foot bass boat with a chart recorder and a really big outboard, put it on my Visa.

Since you seem determined to go ahead with this trip, let me add to what you have told me everything that I know about landlocked salmon.

The main thing I've found is that they don't get nearly as much press as their more glamorous sea-run cousins. In *The Salmon*, however, J. W. Jones does devote a few paragraphs to theorizing why landlocks got landlocked. He draws on the observations of a guy named Ward, who studied the phenomenon of landlocking when a power dam in Washington created Lake Shannon and, consequently, a new population of landlocked sockeyes. The salmon tried to find a way downstream, but were turned back—not by the dam itself but by low water and warm temperatures. The fish retreated to the cold depths of the lake, where they lost the urge to migrate.

Having reported that, I realize I've done nothing to advance your practical (i.e., how-to-catch) knowledge of the landlocked salmon. All I can really do is wish you good luck.

Apprehensively,

Philip

Harpswell, ME

Dear Philip,

You were right, except Art was already waiting when I got to L.L. Bean, which is probably all that kept me off the park benches. Being observed prevents a true shopping frenzy from developing. Even so, having been away from fly fishing for ten years, I was grabbing stuff with both hands and my eyes closed—flies, fly boxes, tools, waders, shoes, and a new reel and line for my old bamboo Orvis. The rod was treated as a curious antique by the salesmen, who kept calling one another over to see it.

On the five-hour drive from Freeport to the river, I learned more from Art about our fish. They look like seafaring salmon in the development stage, called "grilse" when they come in after their first year at sea. Landlocks aren't as great a table fish, Art feels, but then he doesn't think any freshwater fish matches up with those from salt; I suspect he's never eaten walleyes. Anyway, landlocked salmon flesh is white, not pink, the minimum keeper is fourteen inches, and spinning gear is used as commonly (and legally) as the fly rod.

Got my first look at the river from the car ten miles before we reached camp. It looked reassuringly smooth. Got my second look a minute later, and it was still smooth enough, but a yellow raft full of guys in wet suits and crash helmets went tearing past at just a little less than the speed of light. The road, as well as the campsite where we found John's pop-up, is owned by a paper company. Huge trucks loaded with logs careen by from time to time as an added hazard, and there is a metal barrel on wheels near our spot with DANGER: BEAR TRAP lettered on the side.

On the camper was a note: "Am at the Holbrook, looking

for supper. John." Art had his rod case out of the car while I was still reading this. I barely had time to notice that, while the place is quite primitive—no electricity or telephones—the woods are rather open. There's birch and a variety of evergreens, but not much underbrush. Holbrook is the name of one of the pools we'll be fishing. This evening Art and John ferried me 150 yards across it. The current was even stronger than I'd imagined, and the rapids above and below the pool even noisier. Each paddle stroke John took from the stern, and each one he instructed Art to make in the bow, was calculated and precise; seeing them work got rid of some of my tension.

Still, I was happy to have my feet under me while I tried to recover a fly-casting technique that was never more than five on a scale of ten; nor was I back up to three when, watching my Adams drift past on the surface, suddenly I had a fish. It was a beautiful little 10-inch brook trout, and catching it delighted me more than I'd anticipated, until I realized this was because the rest of my tension about the river was gone.

Hell, I loved this river. The constant roar of the rapids, which started twenty yards below me, was great.

The pull of the current against my new waders was invigorating. I'm ready for salmon, and ready for bed. Will write again when I get back to the coast.

Love,

Dad

Dear Philip,

The second morning I caught a salmon. I'd walked a mile up the bank, enjoying the spray and the smell of balsam, casting now and then, till I reached a pool called the Little Eddy, which is big enough to hold a couple of kidney-shaped football fields, and very deep. There's a rock ledge that goes sixty yards up the north edge, from which I could cast and cover maybe two percent of the water, but fish were rising within range.

A small hatch was on, and I scooped up one of the fluttering creatures it consisted of, something with brown wings and a white body. Naturally, the closest I could come from my L.L. Bean collection had white wings and a brown body. I decided not to use it. John had given me a generous number of flies he'd tied for the trip, among them an Atlantic salmon fly called a Bomber. It looks like a bit of horse dung tied to a size-8 hook. "Salmon like it dry," John had said, "they don't like it wet." It was close to the wing color of the insect I'd looked at.

I kept it dry, and on the fourth cast a fish hit and dove that made my recent brook trout seem insincere. "Landlocked salmon are a strong fish," Art had told me, but I was amazed to see, from the first of many leaps, that my fish wasn't more than seven inches long. I put him back, and many more like him in the next four days.

The biggest salmon I caught came, as the books had predicted, out of the roughest water I fished. Again, it was off a rock ledge, and I was using the Bomber again, mostly because it was big enough to see when cast directly into the rapids. This fish hooked himself and ran in that fast water so strongly I was sure I'd lose him, fishing at my mentor's advice with a 2-pound test tippet on my leader.

The tackle held, and I beached my fish on the rocks. He looked enormous.

Just then Art came along with his canvas Orvis creel, which has a ruler printed on it. We measured, and I had a 15-incher, and Art a couple more like it. But at camp we compared Art's creel ruler with a metal one John keeps and found that the canvas had shrunk greatly during the years, the ruler with it, so my fish was thirteen inches now.

So, in five days of fishing long hours, I didn't catch a legal landlocked salmon, but I sure did eat one. Judge, he was delicious.

John had caught four legal fish, Art two. They were disappointed, and it didn't help to notice that the guy at the next campsite had so many big salmon he was smoking the excess ones. We introduced ourselves, of course, and inquired about his method. "Well," he said, "I tie these." And the thing he held out for us to see looked more like a cigarette than a trout fly—a long, white cylinder of clipped deer hair with red stripes down each side, nothing like my now-bedraggled Gray Ghosts, but clearly far more resembling a smelt in the view of a fish.

If I can't find a Rapala or something that looks like that

next time, there'll be nothing for it but to buy, well, let's see: fly-tying kit, plenty of deer hair, extra-long hooks, white lacquer, illustrated book on smelt . . . have I survived the river only to be borne by treacherous currents into the jaws of L.L. Bean on my way back to Miami?

Love,
Dad

Homestead, IA

Dear Dad,

I see that I have failed utterly in trying to act as a stabilizing influence from afar. Maybe I can go with you next time. Get two of everything at Bean's just in case.

Love,
Philip

Cutthroat Business

From *Fly Fishing Through the Midlife Crisis*

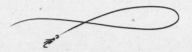

HOWELL RAINES

If you like fly fishing, there will come a time when you want to penetrate to the heart of the sport. Then you are likely to find yourself landing at an airport in Montana or Wyoming. In our case, it was Butte, the birthplace of Evel Knievel, the site of the world's largest open-pit copper mine and the best place to rent a car that will take you to the Big Hole River, which was where Susan, the boys and I found ourselves headed one day in August.

How Susan came to be on that trip is an interesting question, and I'm not sure I know the entire answer. She ordered waders, boots and a fishing vest from L.L. Bean and signed up for Mark Kovach's one-day class. Mark ridiculed me for sending her out with a battered Orvis rod and tried to turn her head with a Powell rod he happened to have for sale. Then

Dick produced a Teton five-weight from his vast collection of seldom-used rods and announced that Susan should take it west. Teton is a small rod company, then located in Idaho, and its advertising projected a kind of latter-day hippie irreverence. That particular Teton was finished in surfboard purple, and it was about the sexiest-looking fly rod you ever saw. Susan said it would do.

This was the summer of 1990. Ben had finished his sophomore year in the film school at NYU, and Jeff had graduated from high school and was getting ready to go off to Colorado State in the fall. I remember Susan saying at some point that this would probably be our last vacation together as a family. I think we both believed that, and not just because our sons were leaving home.

Selectivity is a problem in the West. It is big, and it is full of rivers that are legendary in the sport. In Montana alone, there are the Big Hole, the Bighorn, the Missouri and the Blackfoot, which is no longer what it was but has a kind of holy status as the setting of *A River Runs Through It*. Then, in Wyoming, you have the Yellowstone, the Madison, the Gallatin and the glorious Snake, which actually becomes better when you cross into Idaho and get two Snakes, the South Fork and the Henry's Fork. What the best of these streams have in common is that they have more fish in a mile than you'll find in an entire county back East.

The boys and I had the typical Easterner's response. We wanted to eat the whole thing. Susan, being lower on the fanaticism curve, prevailed on us to accept an itinerary that called for concentrating on a few pieces of quality water. We would hit the Big Hole, the Yellowstone and Madison in Yellowstone Park, the Snake at Jackson Hole, and then wind up with a week of wilderness fishing at a guest ranch on the Gros Ventre River.

On the Big Hole, our guides were a couple of *Rancho Deluxe* types named Wayne Clayton and Stuart Decker, who work out of the Complete Fly Fisher, a fly shop and lodge at Wise River Junction. From their headquarters in an Airstream trailer they called "The Aluminum Love Tube," they played the Western Wildman game very hard. On their days off, they went fishing. As soon as the tourist season ended on the Big Hole, they took off for British Columbia for steelhead. They liked to fly fish. "I'd better. I gave up a wife, a house and a car to do it," said Wayne.

He, in particular, was full of arcane social strategies and droll information. His response to the AIDS crisis was to date nurses on the theory that they got a lot of blood tests. He said he won a lot of money playing golf with his boyhood friend Evel Knievel, because Knievel played poorly and had never learned not to bet against a sure thing. In other words, Wayne said, Knievel was no better at hitting golf balls than he was at staying on motorcycles. Wayne specialized in fishing small dry flies for big brown trout in shallow water that most of the other guides passed up, and I remember him for guiding me to one of the most memorable fish I've ever caught. It was an eighteen-inch brown that was bigger than anything I had ever raised on a dry fly, and I resisted the South Sauty heave and struck the hook perfectly. Just perfectly. I knew it and so did the guide, and Wayne punctuated the moment by shouting *"El grande marrón"*—Spanish for "big brown"—as the fish boiled out into the current and took off.

That was the day I began to understand the kind of fishermen Ben and Jeff were becoming.

"We're going to have fun today," whooped Stuart as soon as he got them into his raft. "These guys can cast."

Wayne, who was in the boat with me, looked across the water at Jeff. "That boy has a beautiful backcast," he said. "Of course, the front end doesn't look so good."

It did after a day of Stuart's coaching on long-distance casting. He taught both Ben and Jeff to double-haul, a technique of pulling, or "hauling," on the line in midcast, so as to increase the velocity with which it moves through the air, thereby increasing the distance that the line can travel on the cast. By the end of the day with Stuart, they were carving the air with long powerful strokes that looked like scenes from instructional films. Both boys now speak reverently of that day as a watershed experience in their fishing careers. For the next three weeks, we heard an astonishing number of sentences beginning with "Stuart says . . ."

In one particularly productive stretch of the Big Hole, I was indulging my weakness for watching birds rather than my fly when I heard Wayne shout, "Set the hook!" I obeyed on reflex and was fast to my biggest fish of the trip, a brown trout of nineteen inches. After releasing this beautiful and totally undeserved fish, I said to Wayne, "Now I can ask the question I was about to ask when that fish struck. Is that a water ouzel over there?"

In Western fishing, I found the birdlife a constant threat to my concentration. I developed a particular fondness for ouzels, humble robin-sized birds that make their living by walking on stream bottoms. In the category of magisterial birds of prey, we saw plenty of ospreys and bald eagles. But nothing beat the sight of white pelicans, summer visitors who rode the rapids of the turbulent Yellowstone with a goofy aplomb.

It had been more than twenty years since I had driven through the Rockies, and I had forgotten how fully they confirm the saying that the true joy of pursuing trout is that they live in such beautiful places. That is doubly true of the area where the borders of Montana, Idaho and Wyoming come together in a slightly cockeyed intersection.

The views along the twenty-mile section of the Snake that runs beside the Tetons are simply supernal. Like the Big Sur coast, this is one of those American spots of such intensely concentrated beauty as to make one say, "Yes, this is it. Bury me here." Elsewhere, the routine beauty of lodgepole pines, granite escarpments and red rock canyons inspires the happy feeling of being time-warped onto the set of a John Ford western.

We certainly owe U. S. Grant our thanks for preserving the Union, but for my money, his best single day's work took place on March 1, 1872, when he created Yellowstone National Park. There are 3,472 square miles in the park, and if you get out while the RV owners are still snug in their bunks, the old gods still rule.

That was underscored for me one morning when my sons and I were casting for cutthroat—the handsome coppery trout that is indigenous to the Rockies—at a spot on the Yellowstone River called Buffalo Ford. This area, near the Yellowstone Lake Lodge, is one of the most popular fly-fishing areas in the park, yet that morning might have been the one the world began.

We had the entire stream to ourselves except for a brown beast that lumbered out of the lodgepole pines, waded into the deep main channel and then swam like a huge dog until it reached the eastern shore about fifty yards below Ben's fishing spot.

"Well, I guess we know why they call it Buffalo Ford," he said.

Rapids-shooting pelicans and swimming buffalo add spice to a fly-fishing outing. Even so, it's hard to upstage the Yellowstone cutthroat, whose original Latin name, *Salmo clarki lewisi*, honored the two explorers who brought their "corps of discovery" here in 1806.

The six miles of catch-and-release water immediately north of Yellowstone Lake is teeming with these handsome fish. I know of no better spot for building the ego of the beginning fly fisher or making the middling fly fisher feel like an expert.

Get there just after the mid-July opening, cast a number 16 Parachute Adams or Caddis with reasonable delicacy, and something stimulating will happen.

Later in the season, the fish get smarter, but cutthroat are the innocents of the trout world. So much so that many accomplished anglers denigrate them. Indeed, the Yellowstone cutts can be pushovers. One day, I had three strikes from the same fish, pricking it sharply each time with the hook, before I finally got it on the fourth take.

But for those who think all cutthroat are dumb, there is Flat Creek, just outside Jackson in the vast meadow at the National Elk Refuge. Flat Creek is noteworthy for several reasons. One, it is the only catch-and-release stream in Wyoming, a state that has been unconscionably slow to protect its trout from people who regard a frying pan as an essential part of their gear.

Secondly, it is good for one's humility, after the pushover fishing on the Yellowstone, to meet the smarter cousins of *Salmo clarki lewisi*. The Snake River finespot cutthroat who live in Flat Creek are as spooky as any Eastern brown trout, and it is good for one's humility to watch them streak away in fits of survivalist terror the moment a fly touches the water. This is what serious fly casters call "highly technical fishing," and a little of it goes a long way.

By the time we set out from Jackson for the South Fork of the Snake River just across the border in Idaho, Susan was beginning to feel that all the fishing was a little too technical.

She had been content to practice her casting and laugh about missed strikes on the Big Hole and Yellowstone. Now she wanted to catch a fish. Luckily, she and Ben were guided on the South Fork by Tom Montgomery, a Massachusetts man who got the fly-fishing bug at Middlebury College and went west to find acclaim as a wildlife photographer, fishing writer and, by most accounts, the best fisherman in Jackson Hole.

It was a superb day for dry fly fishing from the locally made boats marketed as South Fork Skiffs, and under Tom's tutelage Susan brought three fish to hand, including one legitimate trophy of over sixteen inches. "By the end of that day, I was beginning to feel like a fisherman," she recalled later.

Meanwhile, Jeffrey and I were being guided by Paul Brunn, a former Jackson Hole city councilman who is the godfather of the local fishing industry. If they gave doctorates in reading the water and selecting flies, Paul would have one.

Paul's technique with people who are serious about their fishing involves relentless coaching. "Put a cast in that slick spot behind the boulder. Leave it. Leave it. Now strip in line. Strip, strip, strip. Your fly is dragging. Pick it up and go again. Just in front of that willow. Strip, strip, strip." And so on.

Either the person in the front seat of Paul's boat will learn a hell of a lot about reading the water and getting a drag-free float, or he or she will have a strong desire to throttle the guide. At midday, after Jeff had been in the front seat for a few hours banging casts into every target, Paul Brunn said, "How old are you?"

"Eighteen," said Jeff.

"If I had been able to cast like that at your age, I would be a world-class fisherman today," Paul said.

Paul did not get so worked up about my skills. Still, the high point of my day came when he spotted a big cutthroat that was "lit up." That is to say, the fish was literally glowing—a phenomenon that occurs frequently with saltwater fish such as marlin but is rarer in freshwater species. The luminescence signals that the fish is in a feeding frenzy.

Indeed, this particular fish was rising regularly. But it was tucked in behind a willow along a sheer bank in a way that made it almost impossible to reach with a delicate cast. Anyway, it rejected all our standard mayfly and grasshopper imitations. Finally, Paul concluded that the fish was taking nymphs so tiny as to be invisible to the naked eye. He tied a fly no larger than a pinhead to my tippet, and with one clean cast, I had the trout.

"Your old man is a pretty good fisherman," he said to Jeff by way of congratulating me on the accuracy of my casting. I swelled with pride, though we all knew that I would never have taken that trout on my own. But I did not argue with the man. He was an expert at the business of catching cutthroats. I figured he ought to have his say.

Father and Son
Share a Moment at the Dump

From *Zipping My Fly*

RICH TOSCHES

For every little boy who falls in love with fly-fishing there is a man who made it possible, a kind and gentle man who saw the flame and kindled it. For me, it was a guy who went by the name Lucky and hung out near the liquor store in my hometown and always asked me to rub his feet.

No, really, for me it was my father, Nick. He never fly-fished a day in his life, looking at the delicate nine-foot rod and thinking, "Now there's something you're gonna slam in the damn car door, for chrissakes!"

But my father was always behind me. In my pursuit of sports and my pursuit of writing and, frankly, in my pursuit of anything. He was a newspaper editor in Massachusetts for four decades and gave me my first job, which consisted of scraping the sticky paper off the composing-room floor with a putty knife. That was thirty-eight years ago.

He still owes me $24.75.

Today he's retired, spending part of each day reading several newspapers, clipping out articles, and sending them to me in the fervent belief that I might find a way to change a word here and there and turn them into my own columns for my newspaper in Colorado Springs so I could be out of the office by noon every day.

He is a wise, wise man.

And when he did indeed purchase that $15 fly rod from his friend Porky Ferrara—okay, I didn't steal it—he backed up the gesture by looking at his goofy twelve-year-old kid the next day and asking, "So now what?"

And then he'd drive me to the lake or the pond where I learned how to catch bluegills on a popper or perhaps fall off the dam when the trout struck the dry fly, and later to the West River, where he'd drop me off with my fly rod and my waders and offer words of encouragement such as "Don't drown, for chrissakes!"

Sometimes he'd stay and watch—mesmerized, I think, by the sight of his young boy and the graceful motion of the fly rod, the line slicing through the air alongside a New England stream. You could sense the emotion in his voice when he'd shout, "For chrissakes, you're gonna put your eye out with that thing!"

And then he'd leave, probably heading back to the newspaper office for a few hours of work as I stayed and learned the graceful art of fly-fishing.

And most of the time he'd remember to come back and pick me up.

The summer that I got the fly rod, my father asked if I'd like to take a trip with him. Maybe we'd drive up to Maine, he said. And so he bought a huge blue-and-white canvas tent, stuffed it into the trunk of his 1967 Mercury—the fly rod had a safe spot on the backseat—and the two of us left on a ten-day road trip, an adventure that still lingers in my mind today, a magical journey of a young boy and a father who didn't know it when they set out that first day, but who were linked by a powerful bond: Neither of them had any idea how to put up a tent.

The trip brought us north out of Boston along the rugged coast and into Portland, where we turned inland through Lewiston to the town of Mexico—yes, there is an actual place called Mexico, Maine—where we stopped for lunch. We both had the special: moose burritos.

It was right after lunch that we came upon the most exciting thing I had ever seen that did not have a centerfold stapled into the middle of it. It was the Androscoggin River, which combines the native Maine Indian words *Andro* ("land") and *scoggin* ("that L.L. Bean hasn't purchased yet").

The Androscoggin was wider and deeper and faster than any river I had ever seen. It was wide enough that I could not throw a stone across it, although I kept trying until the guy fly-fishing on the opposite shore yelled, "Hey, you little bastard!"

I had no clue whatsoever as to how to fly-fish such a place, a river fast enough and deep enough that I knew only one thing: If I even tried to put my waders on, signaling that I was going to enter the water, my father would have tackled me and thrown me into the trunk with the tent.

So I left the waders in the car and rigged up my fly rod, choosing a large black woolly bugger and adding a couple of split shot. I cast and cast for more than an hour without a strike, and then, suddenly, as the streamer swung toward the bank in the heavy current, the rod doubled and nearly came out of my hands. A huge fish moved out into the current and headed downstream, and because I had never felt anything so powerful, I clamped my fingers onto the fly line and heard the eight-pound test leader snap.

It had all happened so fast I hadn't even yelled. I walked back to the car, where my father had a map opened on the hood, and told him I'd lost one.

"Yeah?" he asked, looking up. "You probably horsed him."

"Ah, horse this," I was thinking, although I did not actually say that to him. I know that because I am still alive, writing this book.

But as I took the fly rod apart and set it on the backseat and climbed back into the front with my dad, my hands still trembled from that brief encounter with a big trout. As we headed out of the town of Mexico and turned onto Highway 142, passing through the small Maine towns of Carthage and Madrid, I remember having this thought—a powerful thought that would lead me into a lifetime of passionate fly-fishing: "Mexico? Carthage? Madrid? Where the hell are we?"

Anyway, we drove on in the Mercury, which was so big we could have pitched tent in it before we'd left the house. Turns out that wouldn't have been a bad idea. In the late afternoon we pulled into the town of Rangeley, which my dad said he'd found earlier on the map and had actually been *trying* to find. I believed him, which was quite a milestone in our relationship.

I'd doubted him on all travel-related matters since a few years earlier when, on a car trip to Florida with three kids stuffed in the backseat, he ran out of gas on a Georgia cotton plantation. After walking quite a distance to a house and finding no one home—he let me walk along with him despite the fact I was only eight, probably in case they had a big dog—he left a five-dollar bill under a rock on the doorstep and filled a big can with gasoline from a pump near the barn.

After the long walk back, he poured the gasoline into the tank and cranked up the Pontiac. I can still remember turning in the backseat to watch the billowing cloud of black smoke that poured from the exhaust pipe as he drove away that day—and reminding myself that when I got big and had my own car, I would never, ever pour two gallons of diesel fuel into it like my daddy had just done.

I told him later that I saw the word *diesel* handwritten on the pump by the barn, but didn't know what it meant. My dad, kind and understanding at all times, was even more so in critical times such as this. When I told him about seeing that "diesel" word on the pump, I remember him looking at me with those understanding eyes and saying, "Jesus Christ, you coulda said something, for chrissakes, dammit to hell!"

Somehow, we made it to Miami, where we spent two terrific weeks, a million memories tucked away in the mind—although for me, about 900,000 of those memories are of watching my father walk along the beach dressed in shorts, black shoes, and black socks.

Anyway, we were in Maine now and pulled into the town of Rangeley during the late afternoon. We stopped at the general store in the little town and bought a couple of sodas. Dad explained to the man behind the counter that we were on a fishing and camping trip. Dad inquired about nearby campgrounds and then asked what there might be to do around town.

"Well," the old man said from behind the counter. "You could go out to the dump and watch the beahs!"

This was Mainese, and meant "bears."

I thought this was a great idea: Let's take the twelve-year-old awkward kid down to the dump to play with the bears.

First, however, there was the simple matter of pitching the tent. So we worked together, both of us huffing and puffing and pulling on this and pulling on that, and surprisingly, within half an hour we had the tent out of the truck.

We spread it on the ground at the campsite, turning it so the door faced the picnic table. Then dad looked at the gigantic pile of aluminum poles on the ground. Then he looked at me. Then we both looked back at the pile of tent poles. If we had any sense at all, we would have stuffed everything back into the trunk and gone home.

We started messing around with the poles, which slid in and out of other poles and went through Flap A and connected to Center Pole D and Awning Support F—although a lot of that information came the following week when we got home and read the instruction booklet, which *someone* had left in the basement.

I still have that blue-and-white tent. It's in my garage, in the original box. And almost every summer my kids make me take it out and we set it up in the backyard and they sleep in it.

I've told them the history of the tent, and now, whenever we begin setting it up, one of my two lovely sons will say, "Look, I'm Grandpa!" and then he'll kick the pile of poles across the yard and yell, "Dammit to hell!"

Oh, how we laugh.

Anyway, somehow my dad and I got the tent set up. It took about three hours. And at dusk, with camp set, we got back into the car and headed for the Rangeley Town Dump, which was about five miles up a dirt road. And within ten minutes of our arrival, the black bears came out of the woods. Six of them.

My father, Mr. Newspaper Guy, reached into the backseat and pulled out his always-ready camera, which did not have any type of telephoto lens, and said I should get out and take some pictures.

I am not kidding.

Once I was outside, with the bears some fifty feet away rifling through the garbage, my father, who stayed in the Mercury, actually said this:

"Get closer!"

A few weeks later, the *Milford Daily News* ran a photograph of bears at a dump in Rangeley, Maine. The credit line read *"Daily News* photo by Richard Tosches." In the photo, one of the bears was very close and you could see it holding its head up, sniffing the air.

Almost as if he had caught the scent of urine in a twelve-year-old kid's pants.

We stayed near Rangeley for three days and discovered gigantic Rangeley Lake. I caught a few trout on my fly rod, Dad caught a few more with his spinning outfit, and we ate trout over the campfire at night. I do not like the taste of trout. I have not eaten one since that night in Maine in 1967. In the years since, we've had a lot of conversations about this idea of catch-and-release. Dad still keeps a trout or two when he fishes and I'm okay with that. But he cannot understand why I release every trout I catch.

"They're good eatin'," he'll say. "Why the hell would anyone go fishing if they won't eat 'em?"

I tell him I do it because I love being in the water, that I love the feeling of being in pristine places where wild trout swim, that I love watching a big trout rise to the surface and sip the tiny fly, perhaps one I have created myself, and feeling the thrill of the fight on the delicate fly rod. I tell him I love knowing that if I do everything just right, I get to watch a large rainbow slide into my net.

"Yeah," he'll say, in that kind and caring way. "I guess I know what you mean.

"Although you could still eat him."

rainbow trout.

From *Catch and Release*

Mark Kingwell

Fishing Is Stupid

I came to fishing late in life. That is, if you can say I came to it at all. Some men are born fishers, some have fishing thrust upon them. Others run screaming when fishing comes calling.

I enjoyed no early bonding experiences fishing with my father, for example. There were no tense Brad Pitt–Tom Skerritt exchanges leavened by an afternoon of gorgeous casts and triumphant landings. There were no Papa-esque hikes into the backcountry to find idyllic wisdom and new insight about the place of men in the world.

No. In fact, the only vivid memory I have of fishing with my father when I was a boy is a pathetic incident somewhere in the backwaters of Prince Edward Island. Ordered to fetch a tackle box that we'd forgotten, I slipped on the bank and fell, cracking the lid of the green metal container in the process and somehow managing to get myself hooked and tangled in spinners and line to such an extent that I could neither move nor cry out for help. It was as if a malevolent spirit resident in the box had been liberated and emerged, hungry for revenge. Minutes or hours later, my irritated father, an Air Force navigator, came along and found me there, bleeding, immobile, and humiliated. One nineteenth-century writer suggested that the essential trait of a good angler is talent at philosophy, by which he meant an ability to extricate a mislaid hook from nose or lip without losing one's temper. I think of this early experience as an opportunity lost, but I came to philosophy anyway and fishing not at all. Perhaps it was because I lacked another important angler's quality, perseverance. I conceded defeat. The tackle box was bigger than whatever amount of character I had managed to build.

Since then, I have come across a surprising number of otherwise functional and well-adjusted men who tell similar stories. Wayward casts. Dropped catches. Snapped lines. Lures or spoons gouged deeply into palms, legs, faces. Also, fathers and brothers and pets mistakenly hooked. Eyes injured, tackle lost, lectures endured. We have been yelled at and laughed at. We are a sad bunch, existing without benefit of talk-show sympathy or support group, a scarred and bitter crew who cannot stomach the idea of fishing and, inwardly, resent the domineering, impatient fathers who made us this way.

And our only armour is psychic—namely, the unspoken yet

firm conviction that fishing is stupid. Ed Zern speaks for all of us in his short but heartfelt memoir *To Hell with Fishing*. The key to fishing, as any angler will tell you, is *thinking like a fish*. What would the fish do? What does it want to eat? Where would it look? "Of course," says Zern, "the reason a fish thinks the way he does is that his brain is very tiny in relation to his body. So the tinier the fisherman's brain the easier it is for him to think like a fish, and catch trout right and left."

Or, as I would more elegantly express it, *fishing is stupid*.

Who Is Fred?

Fred is Sean's best friend and fishing buddy. He is, you might say, Batman to Sean's Robin, if for no other reason than he has all the gear, the ultimate angling utility belt. Fred owns every piece of fishing equipment ever devised by man to aid in the uneven battle between twenty-first-century human technology and the pea-brained but feisty trout. When Fred unloads his truck, he looks like Arnold Schwarzenegger getting ready for the last ten minutes of the movie.

Fred impresses me for many reasons, not least that he has the jangling, laden vest of the experienced angler. And watching Fred tie flies in the cabin, his clamp set on the table after the dinner dishes have been cleared away, is mesmerizing and humbling. Tiny barbless hooks, hardly more than twists of wire; silk thread and pheasant feather; hackles and wings and beads; the subtle details of color and size and shape. All minutely detailed to mimic a mayfly larva or full-grown mosquito or midge. Fred swirls and winds the thread, adds a feather, takes a feather away, and finishes the microscopic masterpieces with a practiced flourish of knotting. A perfect green nymph ready for the leader. I think: I'll never be able to do that—that little flick and pinch with the tying key that rounds off the threading and makes the fly whole.

Flies themselves are lovely things, useful but beautiful in their purpose, gorgeous when displayed in leather books or under glass cases, the multi-hued machinery of death. Most of them have traditional names that, especially in the English lexicon, mention their entomological origins or distinctive silhouettes: Hare's Ears, the Lead-Winged Coachman, Olive Quill, Iron-Blue Dun, Dotterel Dun, Honey-Dun Hen Hackle, the Blue Hawk. Sometimes, as with the Dr. Cahill or Tupp's Indispensable, they allude, not very clearly, to some early practitioner of the art of fly-tying. Just as the British, in contrast to their more overt North American cousins, tend to favour ironic or genteel names for other violent machines—who else, for example, would call a fighter plane a Pup, a Camel, or a Dart?—so their fly names remain archaic and Waltonian. American innovations, by contrast, tend to bear names like Terminator and Slayer, which somehow seem to violate the genteel spirit of fly-fishing, whatever the similar outcome of a landed trout. Or is it maybe American straight-forwardness over English hypocrisy?

Anyway, the language of flies exhibits the same combination of elegance and ferocity that underwrites the sport more generally, not to mention that pleasing cadence of expertise causally deployed. G.E.M. Skues, for example, compares two similar flies in a passage of swooning impenetrability from his classic *The Way of a Trout with a Fly* (1924): "Each has a peacock herl body. The dun of the starling wings in the Coachman is reproduced by the dun centre of the hackle of the Little Chap, and the red hackle of the Coachman by the red points of the hackle of the Little Chap. But if they be dressed on the same size of hook, when one will kill, as a general proposition the other will kill." To which the only reasonable duffer's response is, *I believe you*.

Despite his many virtues, Fred's presence on the fishing weekends violated the implicit Kingwells-only policy, not to mention complicating our two-men-to-a-boat logistics. But this turned out to be good news for everybody, and not just because his grilled prawns and pesto linguine went down so well after a day on the lake. He also had the outsider's ability to put moronic family conflicts into context, so that the nightly games of Hearts—that meanest of childish card games—did not degenerate into the shouting matches and semi-serious shoving that might otherwise have come from the combination of four hyper-competitive Kingwells and a little too much wine over dinner. These cheery card games always threaten to become all too reminiscent of the ugly Trivial Pursuit free-for-alls of the 1980s or the hockey-watching debacles of the early 1990s. Nobody really wanted a repeat of these scenes; they make it hard to go out fishing together the next day.

Growing up with two brothers, the three of us separated by six years, there was always a fair amount of blood from routine boyhood violence. We all have the fine network of scar tissue on our hands and knees and elbows from cuts and slashes and jabs that are a part of a life's ascent into manhood. There were also a couple of spectacular injuries. The summer I was nine, a recoiling air-rifle handle caught me in the right eye and sliced open my eyelid—one of those small cuts that releases a terrifying stream of blood, which seeped through my fingers and down my face. I remember running home, and then sitting next to my mother in her car while she, cigarette in her mouth and panic in her heart because she thought I'd lost an eye, frantically drove me to the hospital on the Air Force base where we lived. One stitch on the eyelid was enough, but neither of us had known that during the worst car ride of my life, me with a blood-soaked tea towel pressed to my eye.

And there was the time Sean, in another military house in another part of the country, en route from the downstairs fridge where the soft drinks were stored, slipped on some water I had spilled on the basement floor. He was about eleven. Falling, he hit the exposed concrete with the bottle still cradled in his left arm, smashing it and driving a big knife-like wedge of glass deep into his forearm. Upstairs I heard the crash and said to myself, in my best Howard Cosell interior voice, *Down goes Kingwell! Down goes Kingwell!* Then I heard the panicked yelling. His gash is still the nastiest and most shocking laceration I have seen up close; it went bone-deep across the diagonal width of his arm. And every time I see the snake of untannable scars on his arm—the cut itself plus long surgical incisions to repair nerve damage—I think of that open mouth of dark red muscle on the white flesh, the fear in his eyes as he came running up the basement steps.

I got hit by a car the day I graduated high school, riding my bike down Wellington Crescent in Winnipeg, and that was a nasty spill, all right, with long cuts from the car's grille down my left calf and across my right knee, and a layer of skin torn off most of my right thigh where the loose bike shorts I was wearing rode up, my leg scraping across asphalt as I slid to a stop in the middle of the road. The impact almost, but not quite, broke my left leg; instead the leg swelled up to twice its normal size, sporting a gruesome purple contusion that faded and kaleidoscoped to various greens and yellows over the next few weeks of couch-riding convalescence. That was bad, and stupid, too, since I wasn't wearing a helmet, but it didn't really *hurt* except for a dismal half hour lying on an emergency-room gurney as the shock wore off and it felt like someone was carefully plying the length of my leg with hot knives.

The injury I remember most, however, was the time Steve, that shameless goon, the Kim Clackson of the sandlot and backyard, broke my arm. He denies this, of course, but the facts are pretty clear. Under the crude basketball hoop we had bolted above the garage door at the house in Winnipeg, playing lazy one-on-one on the wet tarmac, he fouled me so hard on an outside jumpshot that I came down with my ass well back of my feet. I fell backward and instinctively stuck out my arms to break the fall, in the process hyperextending and jamming the fibula of my left one. A greenstick fracture, when the bone doesn't actually break but sort of buckles and twists in the middle like a young branch. It hurt like hell, though, a low throb that built slowly over the next hour to unignorable pain. Steve laughed when I told him I wanted to go to the hospital. Come to that, he laughed when I fell, too. I had to call our mother at work and ask her to come home and take me to the emergency room.

This kind of overt violence—yes, yes, I know, he denies the whole thing—was fairly unusual for Steve, who was more often an accomplished but subtle rec-room terrorist and after-school bully. In our daily battles over TV channel control, toy appropriation, and basement space, especially as I grew bigger and almost as tall as him, Steve quickly adopted an expansionist foreign policy, backed up with big-stick military intervention. He was expert in the principle of delayed retaliation. Bracing myself for the return shot during one of our frequent tussles, I would see Steve's face suddenly relax into a wintry smile. "Don't worry, Mark," he would say, "I'm not going to hit you *now*. But I *will* get you back, sometime before you go to bed tonight. You won't know when it's coming. But before bed."

Nerves on edge like a hunted animal, I cringed and cowered at his merest feint in my direction as evening slowly became night. Steve was adept at the delays, too—a crucial refinement. Sometimes he would wait until my guard was entirely down, when I was brushing my teeth or saying good night to our parents, and then he would dance in, Ali-style, from the other room and clip me smartly across the back of the head, then juke gleefully out of the way when I tried to hit back. I credit this experience for my later deep understanding of the principle of nuclear deterrence.

Sitting in the boat one morning at the lake, it occurred to me that, all other issues aside, I owe Steve a broken arm.

"You won't know when it's coming, Steve," I whispered softly to myself, slowly hauling line on my last cast. "But sometime soon. Sometime before you die," I pulled the line a few more feet and gave vent to a low cackle of cinematic evil-mastermind laughter. "Talk? No, Mr. Bond. I expect you to *die*."

So, anyway, all in all it was good that Fred was there, a placid presence capable of ensuring minimal civil behavior. But even more than these considerable contributions, Fred fulfilled the ancient and honorable role of *gillie*, the expert semi-outsider whose stores of lake wisdom and common sense make the rest of us look good. Sean, to be sure, has no need of this, being just as accomplished an angler. But Sean is our younger brother, which means that Steve and I cannot possibly listen to him. Fred is the perfect guide, combining a regimental sergeant-major's desire for competence with the Zen-like placidity of a pitching coach.

Like all good anglers, Fred also illustrates the ancient aesthetic maxim that the exercise of skill is an end in itself. Which sounds complicated but isn't. On the other hand, it is *deep*, and in the way sometimes only simple things can be. Which means maybe it's time for a new chapter.

But before that, a story—in the form of a letter from my father. It doesn't illustrate *sprezzatura*, exactly, but it does say something about style:

Hi Mark:
After we were talking I remembered a story. I don't know if you recall, but one time you, Steven, and I drove from Toronto to Quebec to see my parents. I think we were still in Clinton, so you were pretty young. My grandfather's house in the country had been closed up for a while then, but my mother got it opened up so we could spend some time there. There was a little brook that ran through my uncle's place adjacent to my grandfather's and it had (and had had since I was a boy) a nice supply of speckled trout. They came up the brook from Rivière aux Pins, which also ran through my uncle's property in the spring when the water was high, and then got trapped in the pools

when the water went down. They had plenty of food and so grew quite nicely.

I had fished for them when I was a boy, with fishing line tied to a pole cut from the alder bushes, where you shortened your line as required by winding it around the pole, small fish hooks, and fat juicy worms. I wish I could remember how old Steve was, but anyway old enough to want to try his hand. The way I remember him is sitting on the brook bank, with infinite patience dangling his worm in the water while the mosquitoes, which were absolutely awful that summer, tried to eat him alive. Of course, there was no reel on the pole, nor indeed any room, what with the overhanging bushes, to "play" a fish anyway, so if you got a bite, you just tried to yank the fish out of the water.

I remember Steve got a bite and yanked so hard that the fish flew off the hook and up over the telephone lines and landed in the dirt road behind us. Still another kind of fishing, I guess you could say.

Love, Dad

I'm sorry to have to report that Steve, though undeniably stylish in other respects, not least his complement of Brooks Brothers suits, has advanced his angling technique only marginally since then. He still has a tendency to slap his backcast on the water behind him. He still tries to horse his fish right out of the water when he's got a bite, dragging a tiny rainbow trout bouncing across the surface of the lake. And if he thinks he has a strike, which is rather more often than evidence and rational judgment would allow, he has perfected a wild attempted hook-set that sends his fly up and out of the water, sailing over our ducking heads.

On the other hand, he has yet to hurl a trout all the way into the dirt. And I suppose you might call that progress.

"Fishing Is Stupid," "Who Is Fred?" from *Catch and Release* by Mark Kingwell, copyright © 2003 by Mark Kingwell. Used by permission of Viking Penguin, a division of Penguin Group (USA) Inc. and Fletcher and Parry LLC.

Real Men and Their Boys

CHUCK BAILEY

Dad was from the old school, a generation of "real men" whose conversational preferences leaned toward sports, weather, work, and the outdoors. I had a greater chance of catching a world-record largemouth than hearing my dad share private feelings and matters of the heart. To get a glimpse of the man inside was a rare and wonderful treat. When such an insight occurred, it usually happened while fishing.

In the pre-dawn darkness it required real "father and son" teamwork to hoist the heavy johnboat up onto the car rack. After wondering why we hadn't done this the night before, we hastily stowed the rest of the gear, and jumped into the old Plymouth.

With the ol' fishin' hole more than an hour away, the driving time gave us a chance to clear away the remaining traces of slumber and to engineer our fishing strategy. The resulting game plan might encompass bass, crappie, bluegills, catfish, even carp. It didn't really matter; we were going "fishin'" and that was all that counted.

After flipping a coin to see who would row first, we eased the boat away from the dock into the early-morning mist. Except for the creaking of an oarlock, we entered into a silent and mystical world, far away from traffic, cars, and telephones. Few words were spoken while the sun's flames melted the cold black-and-white dawn into a warm collage of colors. Our bobbers and doomed worms found their marks next to the lily pads and the stage was set.

And then the magic of a son-and-dad fishing trip began to work in mysterious ways. It would begin with a simple lesson on knot tying, or when to set the hook. But if I waited long enough, Dad would begin to recount stories. One by one the memories were hung upon the stringer until the sunset declared our limit had been filled.

They were stories of long ago, when he was a young lad growing up on the farm in Michigan. I suspect he thought his outdoor yarns were simply about smallmouth and pike fishing, deer hunting, or jigging minnows in Grampa's ice shack, but to me they revealed so much more.

Every story inadvertently exposed secrets of the heart, which "real men" rarely spoke of; special relationships with brothers, or uncles, or friends. If you carefully unfolded each story you could sense the unspoken love and respect between fishing partners and family members.

Though never mentioned, emotions and matters of the heart were the invisible glue binding the bulk of the stories together. Certainly they were not the intended focus of the outdoor tales, but they inevitably disclosed something new about the man I cherished the most, my dad.

Fishing has always been more than just boats, worms, and bobbers. And if the outdoor formula includes fathers and sons, there is something magical about the fishing experience. Longing to reexperience this outdoor magic, I was motivated in the winter of 1994 to place a long-distance telephone call to a Florida guide. A few moments later a reservation was excitedly confirmed for a February fishing reunion for me and my lifetime hero.

Now a middle-aged Northwestern smallmouth fisherman, I drooled as the Southern guide teased me with stories of trophy largemouths submitting to large shiners and balloon bobbers in the reeds, a technique I had always been eager to try. But most of all, I looked forward to hearing Dad tell those stories again. It would be a time to be as close as a "real man" and his son can get.

But the fishing reunion was not to be. Dad died a month later of a massive heart attack. I was numb for weeks. Although my family decided to continue on to Florida that February as originally planned, to see Gramma and visit Disney World, the outdoor portion of the trip had lost its allure.

My first impulse was to cancel my guided fishing trip; after all, the plan was originally designed to be a father-and-son excursion. But as the day grew closer, I had an unexpected change of heart. I was a dad now and it would be a great opportunity to take one of my offspring fishing, to make memories of our own.

And my dad . . . he will always be there. He'll be in the treasured stories I pass on to my kids and grandchildren. Lessons in knot tying, casting, fish handling, and patience will be faithfully passed on to the next eager generation. But the greatest blessings will come when their young hearts peer into the revealing window of their father's stories.

History will continue to reveal to anglers, young and old, that the key ingredient in the mystery and magic of "fishin'" is the stories we share. For whether the stories are factual or a "whopper of a fish story," whether the tales make us laugh or raise a suspicious eyebrow, they do indeed reveal something about the inner person, and that can't help but bring the generations closer together.

A Fishing Father

RON BROOKS

I don't remember many specific Father's Days. As I recall, they took a back seat to other holidays like Christmas, Thanksgiving, and Mother's Day. Maybe it was a macho thing—what man wants a holiday named for him?

But it really didn't matter that it took a back seat. It was still a special day and it still meant finding a gift for my dad. That task was harder than you might think, and it became harder as the years went by.

My dad was a fisherman. I don't mean that he simply liked to fish. I mean—he was a fisherman. He ate, slept, dreamed, and talked about fishing. The most logical gift every year would be something from the fishing world.

Only, I had a problem with these gifts. I don't know about your father, but my father never waited for someone to give him something. He was not one to hint around prior to a holiday in hopes of getting what he wanted as a gift. When he needed or wanted something, he bought it—right then and there. There was a tackle shop, and if it had what he wanted, he bought it. Men seem to be that way. Except for maybe the eBay phenomenon, men usually don't shop; they buy. That was my dad.

Every year that goes by since we lost him makes me appreciate him more, and not for the obvious things, but for things I find myself doing that fall right into his footsteps. It amazes me the influence he had simply by his presence in my life.

Not many fishing trips went by as I was growing up that did not include me in the boat with him. He never really invited me to go with him; it was just sort of understood that I would go. Only after I married and moved away from home did I have a need to buy fishing tackle and equipment. Before that it was common knowledge that his gear was community property, and I used it whenever I wanted.

We fished all over South Florida as I grew up, from Key West to Naples and Palm Beach. Even after I married, I did not buy a boat of my own for several years. I didn't need to have one—I had his.

This Father's Day, I find myself looking at my own kids. Kids? They're all married and my two boys are over thirty. They both love to fish, and as I watch them and their families,

I find myself watching me. I see myself doing the same things my father did with me. I don't really think about it—it's like it was ingrained in my being.

When they were growing kids, the boat seldom left the house without all three of us in it. I bought rods and reels for them, but it was understood that they were "ours."

As they grew older, my boat was always a family thing—not my own possession. My oldest son, Tom, with whom I fish today, used the boat more than I did, it seems. David moved to another state, but he has one of "our" boats that I didn't want to trade, and he fishes out of it every week.

The older each of them gets, the more of me I can see in them. They have kids now, and I watch as Tom takes his son, James, fishing—teaching him everything he learned from me and from my father. David's kids aren't old enough yet, but I'm sure I will see it in him as well.

There's a point somewhere in all this rambling, and I guess it's this: whether you realize it or not, as a father, you have more influence on your children simply by being their father than you can ever imagine. My wife sometimes jokingly says I'm acting more like my father every day. I've already heard Tom's wife tell him he was acting like me.

My father was a loving man; a bit eccentric; a bit impatient; overly cautious; and truthful to a fault. He had no more quirks than any other aging man.

As I think back on how he raised me and what that did for me in life, I have to be thankful. As I look at my own kids,

Tom, David, and my daughter Sara, I'm thankful once again, thankful that my father instilled in me something that drove me to raise them the same way he raised me.

Was it the fishing that caused all this? Obviously not, though I could make a pretty good argument for that theory. I think it was that he did what we all need to do as men and fathers. He looked out for his kids. He taught us right and wrong, good and bad, and he did it with a firm, loving hand.

I miss him this week—heck, I miss him every day. I'm celebrating without his physical presence; but the evidence of his life today is as real as it was ten years ago. As you celebrate Father's Day this next week, take a good look at yourself, men. Maybe this isn't a holiday for all of us to receive gifts. Maybe it's a holiday made for us to look within ourselves and see just what kind of father we really are.

We Fish

From *We Fish*

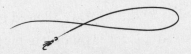

JACK AND OMARI DANIEL

My grandfather stays with my father
because he fishes.
Wading these motherly banks
of the Juniata evokes memory.
Each cast, each fish,
keeps the memory of his father fresh.
This is how we beat death.

I know if Alzheimer's ever claims my
father, as it did his, all I have to do
is fish. I will fish the Juniata, and
let the memories of my father flow
through me. Fishing for channel cats,

doing the Juniata float, and sneaking
down the back side of the church
to fish on Sundays. I will fish
because we fish, and they fished, and
I know my father can never leave me,
if I just fish.

Contributors

Peter Kaminsky writes about fishing and food. He is the author of *The Moon Pulled Up an Acre of Bass*, *The Fly Fisherman's Guide to the Meaning of Life*, and *The Elements of Taste*. His Outdoors column has appeared regularly in the *New York Times* for nearly twenty years and he has been a contributing editor to *Field & Stream*, *Sports Afield*, and *Outdoor Life*.

William G. Tapply is the author of a dozen nonfiction books, twenty-one mystery novels, and hundreds of magazine articles. Fly-fishing is his great love and the subject of several of his nonfiction works. He is a contributing editor for *Field & Stream* magazine and *Upland Almanac*, and a contributing writer for *American Angler*. He has traveled widely throughout New England, up and down the East Coast, and in Canada, the western United States, and the Tropics, mostly in pursuit of fish and fishing stories. He lives in Hancock, New Hampshire, with his wife, Vicki Stiefel, and their sundry animals.

Perie Longo has published two books of poetry: *Milking the Earth* (John Daniel, 1986) and *The Privacy of Wind* (John Daniel, 1997). Her work has appeared in *The Prairie Schooner* and *California State Poetry Quarterly*, among other journals. In 2002, she was nominated for a Pushcart Prize. For twenty years she has led the poetry workshops for the Santa Barbara Writers Conference and leads the annual three-day Santa Barbara Summer Poetry Workshop. She teaches with the California-Poets-in-the-Schools program, and privately. She owes her love of poetry to her father, with whom she often fished.

Neal Karlen is a regular contributor to the *New York Times*, where "The Iceman Fisheth" originally appeared. A former staff writer at *Newsweek* and a contributing editor for *Rolling Stone*, his most recent books were *Shanda: The Making and Breaking of a Self-Loathing Jew* (2004) and *Slouching Toward Fargo*, which won the Casey Award for best baseball book of 2000. He has collaborated with Henny Youngman and Jenny McCarthy on their autobiographies, and with the musician Prince on an unproduced rock opera. He lives in Minneapolis, where he ice-fishes with his father.

Nationally syndicated columnist **W. Bruce Cameron** is the author of *8 Simple Rules for Dating My Teenage Daughter*, which was the basis for the television show *8 Simple Rules* on ABC. His book *How to Remodel a Man* became an instant bestseller upon its release in September 2004. Cameron lives in Santa Monica, California, with his teenage son, who gives him plenty to write about.

Teresa Cader is the author of two collections of poetry. *Guests*, published in 1991 by the Ohio State University Press, won the Norma Farber First Book Award from the Poetry Society of America and *The Journal* Award in Poetry. Her second book, *The Paper Wasp*, was published in 1999 by Northwestern University Press/TriQuarterly Books. A long poem from that book won the George Bogin Memorial Award from the Poetry Society of America. Her work has also been published in *The Atlantic Monthly*, *Poetry*, *Harvard Magazine*, *Slate*, and *Ploughshares*, among other publications. She has won fellowships from the Mary Ingraham Bunting Institute at Radcliffe College, the National Endowment for the Arts, the Massachusetts Cultural Council, the Massachusetts Artists Foundation, the MacDowell Colony, and the Bread Loaf Writers Conference.

When his minor league baseball career with the Los Angeles Dodgers ended in South Carolina in 1974, **Ed Zieralski** took his sore right arm and began throwing words instead of baseballs. He settled in San Diego, where today he is the outdoor writer and golf writer for the San Diego *Union-Tribune*. When he's not fishing, he's out pursuing his other passions—turkey hunting, deer hunting, and golf. He owes his love for life, the outdoors, and golf to his father, Edward J. "Zeke" Zieralski, who took the time to take him on his first fishing trip, on a Delaware River tributary named Crosswick Creek.

Loren Webster is a native of Seattle, Washington, and spent much of his formative years fishing the Puget Sound. Now retired, he considers himself foremost an outdoorsman (though he has been everything from a soldier to a tax preparer), whether fishing and kayaking the waters of the Pacific Northwest or hiking and cross-country skiing the Cascades and Olympics. Although he's written about many things, virtually everything he writes is inspired by his love of nature.

Nelson Bryant is a graduate of Dartmouth College and a twice-wounded paratrooper who served in World War II, making the Normandy and Holland jumps and participating in the Battle of the Bulge. He has worked as a logger, a dock builder, a cabinet-maker, and carpenter, and for fifteen years was the managing editor of the *Daily Eagle* in Claremont, New Hampshire. In 1967, he began writing a hunting, fishing, and outdoors column for the *New York Times*, an endeavor he still pursues, although with reduced frequency. He and his former wife, Jean Morgan Bryant, have two sons, two daughters, and eight grandchildren. He lives on Martha's Vineyard with his companion, Ruth Kirchmeier.

Michael Pearce is currently the outdoor writer/photographer for the Wichita *Eagle*, the largest newspaper in Kansas, and has won many national awards in his twenty-three years in the business. He was previously a full-time freelance writer for nineteen years, with masthead positions with *Outdoor Life* and *The Robb Report*. He also wrote outdoor stories for the leisure and arts page of the *Wall Street Journal* between 1985 and 2000. An avid outdoorsman, he probably spends over a hundred days a year afield, often with his daughter, Lindsey, and his son, Jerrod.

Marc Folco, a New England native, has fished and hunted passionately since he was a young boy. He has written the "Open Season" weekly outdoors column for the *Standard Times* in New Bedford, Massachusetts, since 1988, and his stories have won more than thirty national and New England awards. Folco also has been published in *The Fisherman* and *Muzzleblasts* magazines.

Roger Lee Brown runs a professional bass-fishing school in the Adirondack Mountains in upstate New York. Information about the school can be found at www.capital.net/~rlbrown. His articles on fishing can be viewed at www.probass.com.

Dan Durbin is an outdoor writer from Waukesha, Wisconsin. Along with a weekly outdoors column, he also writes for several regional and national publications. When not writing or running his small advertising agency, he can be found either in a tree stand or casting for bass. Oftentimes, his wife, Lisa, or his sons, Hunter and Blake, will be with him.

A "fisher of men" six days a week, Pastor **Charles (Chuck) Bailey** is a Lutheran minister and an avid bass fisherman on his day off. As the president of Western Bass Club (the oldest bass club in America), he writes to help educate and inspire the next generation of anglers. His articles and love of the outdoors are the blessed results of a dad who once upon a time cared enough to take his son fishing.

Ron Brooks is a freelance outdoor writer with credits in a number of outdoor and fishing magazines. In his role as About.com's saltwater fishing guide (www.saltfishing.about.com), he contributes weekly information and content to assist other saltwater anglers. Ron grew up fishing with his father, and has in turn instilled the love for fishing in his own children. His current project involves doing the same for his grandchildren.

Bibliography and Recommended Reading

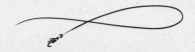

Bourjaily, Vance, and Philip Bourjaily. *Fishing by Mail*. New York: Atlantic Monthly Press, 1993.

Daniel, Jack L., and Omari C. Daniel. *We Fish: The Journey to Fatherhood*. Pittsburgh: University of Pittsburgh Press, 2003.

Dennis, Jerry. *A Place on the Water: An Angler's Reflections on Home*. New York: St. Martin's/Griffin, 1993.

Greenlaw, Linda. *The Lobster Chronicles: Life on a Very Small Island*. New York: Hyperion, 2002.

Hemingway, Jack. *Misadventures of a Fly Fisherman: My Life With and Without Papa*. New York: McGraw-Hill, 1987.

Kaminsky, Peter. *The Fly Fisherman's Guide to the Meaning of Life : What a Lifetime on the Water Has Taught Me about Love, Work, Food, Sex, and Getting Up Early*. Emmaus, Pa.: Rodale, 2002.

———. *The Moon Pulled up an Acre of Bass: A Flyrodder's Odyssey at Montauk Point*. New York: Theia, 2001.

Kingwell, Mark. *Catch and Release: Trout Fishing and the Meaning of Life*. New York: Viking, 2003.

Lang, Andrew. *Angling Sketches*. 1891. Available online at Project Gutenberg: www.gutenberg.org/etext/2022.

Maclean, Norman. *A River Runs Through It and Other Stories*. Chicago: University of Chicago Press, 1976.

McGuane, Thomas. *The Longest Silence: A Life in Fishing*. New York: Knopf, 1999.

Plummer, William. *Wishing My Father Well: A Memoir of Fathers, Sons, and Fly-Fishing*. New York: Overlook Press, 2000.

Quinnett, Paul. *Pavlov's Trout: The Incompleat Psychology of Everyday Fishing.* Kansas City: Andrews McMeel, 1994.

Raines, Howell. *Fly Fishing Through the Midlife Crisis*. New York: Doubleday, 1994.

Tosches, Rich. *Zipping My Fly: Moments in the Life of an American Sportsman*. New York: Perigee, 2002.

Waitzkin, Fred. *The Last Marlin*. New York: Penguin, 2000.